RAND NATIONAL DEFENSE RESEARCH INSTITUTE

T0308508

Building Special Operations Partnerships in Afghanistan and Beyond

Challenges and Best Practices from Afghanistan, Iraq, and Colombia

Austin Long, Todd C. Helmus, S. Rebecca Zimmerman, Christopher M. Schnaubelt, Peter Chalk

Prepared for the Office of the Secretary of Defense

Approved for public release; distribution unlimited

For more information on this publication, visit www.rand.org/t/RR713

Library of Congress Cataloging-in-Publication Data is available for this publication.
ISBN: 978-0-8330-8759-1

Published by the RAND Corporation, Santa Monica, Calif.
© Copyright 2015 RAND Corporation
RAND® is a registered trademark.

Cover photos: Norwegian Naval Special Operations and RAND authors, used with permission.

Support RAND

Make a tax-deductible charitable contribution at
www.rand.org/giving/contribute

www.rand.org

Preface

Building the capacity of Afghan special operations forces (SOF) is a key goal of the United States and its coalition partners. In February and March of 2013, RAND analysts conducted extensive battlefield circulations in Afghanistan and visited multiple training sites for Afghan SOF. The mentors at these sites hailed from a variety of International Security Assistance Force (ISAF) contributing nations, including the United States, Lithuania, Romania, Australia, Norway, and the United Kingdom. This report summarizes key partnering practices drawn from observations of these international partners and presents findings from SOF partnership case studies in Iraq and Colombia. The goal is to identify best practices for SOF partnership that can benefit the development of the Afghan special operations capability. These best practices also have broader applicability for special operations partnerships beyond Afghanistan.

This research was sponsored by the Special Operations Joint Task Force–Afghanistan and conducted within the International Security and Defense Policy Center of the RAND National Defense Research Institute, a federally funded research and development center sponsored by the Office of the Secretary of Defense, the Joint Staff, the Unified Combatant Commands, the Navy, the Marine Corps, the defense agencies, and the defense Intelligence Community.

For more information on the International Security and Defense Policy Center, see http://www.rand.org/nsrd/ndri/centers/isdp.html or contact the director (contact information is provided on the web page).

Contents

Summary

To better understand how the Special Operations Joint Task Force–
Afghanistan (SOJTF-A) and its subordinate units can effectively solid-
ify the capabilities of Afghan special operations forces (SOF), a team
of RAND analysts visited U.S. and coalition units partnering with
Afghan SOF. The team also examined SOF-partnership case studies
from Iraq and Colombia. The goal of this study was to understand
key challenges confronting the SOF partnering mission and identify
best practices for partnering across an array of international units. The
study and its recommendations are focused on partnership efforts in
Afghanistan, which are likely to continue (albeit in a different form)
after 2014, but should be useful to future SOF capacity-building missions as well.

Best Practices for SOF Partnership in Afghanistan

Operations should be subordinated to capability development. A
focus on achieving operational effects with Afghan SOF has superseded the development of Afghan SOF capability. A frequent refrain
in interviews conducted during this study was that Afghan SOF are "a
big pile of muscle," meaning they are tactically proficient but lack "a
nervous system and skeleton," the structures necessary for operational
planning, intelligence collection, logistics, etc. Building Afghan SOF
capability in these areas will require simpler operations and a lower
operational tempo (OPTEMPO). This will be reinforced in the post-
2014 timeframe, as fewer international forces will be present to provide
these functions.

Focus on sustainable operations. Many coalition assets, such as rotary air and intelligence, surveillance, and reconnaissance (ISR), that have supported Afghan SOF will be very scarce or unavailable after 2014. In light of this coming shortfall, planners need to consider the Afghan capability to replace coalition enablers and to begin preparations in present-day operations. In future conflicts, it may be best to keep the end state in mind and limit provisioned assets to only those that can be sustained. This will help avoid some of the challenges that ensue when partnered units must be weaned from coalition enablers.

Deliberately wean Afghan SOF from unsustainable support. Many Afghan commanders interviewed for this study spoke with palpable fear on the issue of coalition force withdrawal. Many of these Afghan officers received little guidance on the speed and timing of the drawdown of mentorship assets. This is no doubt a result of the strategic context, in which such decisions had not yet been made. Without this guidance, fears run wild that support will be removed "cold turkey." This suggests that, in Afghanistan and beyond, there is a need to develop more sustainable operations and OPTEMPO early in the development phase of partner SOF, rather than trying to do so later. Furthermore, U.S. and coalition forces should clearly communicate to partner units how mentorship and support will be withdrawn after 2014. This will give indigenous SOF units the opportunity to plan accordingly; will avoid fears of a sudden, dramatic reduction in support; and will limit the risks of a future rise in attrition.

Link SOF to existing intelligence infrastructure. Intelligence is the lynchpin of special operations, yet in Afghanistan, many units lacked an organic intelligence capability and were thus highly dependent on coalition forces for intelligence. In Afghanistan, there are a variety of existing sources of intelligence, including the National Directorate of Security (Afghanistan's domestic intelligence service), and several U.S. and coalition forces outfits have worked to help connect these intelligence assets with Afghan SOF at the tactical level. Fostering these types of connections will be critically important across all Afghan SOF units, though the challenges are significant as intelligence sharing is not the norm in Afghanistan.

Promote deep partnership through extensive rapport building. Virtually every individual interviewed as part of this report noted that rapport was the critical ingredient to partnership success. Summarizing many of these comments, one officer remarked, "Rapport is everything." Even if this is a bit hyperbolic, it demonstrates the centrality of rapport to partnership. At least six key factors were identified as being helpful in promoting positive rapport with partner units:

1. Units that returned time and time again to work with the same partner unit reported unusually positive rapport.
2. Rapport benefits when mentors engaged in non-transactional relationships with Afghans. This was most frequently expressed as "hanging out."
3. Respect for Afghan culture was critical and was emphasized by a number of Afghan commanders interviewed for this report.
4. Commanders must set a clear intent among subordinates on the need for and importance of rapport.
5. Enhance language capacity of mentors so that they are able to communicate with indigenous SOF counterparts.
6. Where security conditions permit, mentors should live in close proximity to SOF counterparts.

Use mentorship networks and the chain of command to your benefit. Logistics is a perennial problem among Afghan SOF units. A commonly referenced story involves unit S-4s sending resupply requests to higher channels only to never receive the requested materials, sometimes not even a confirmation that the request was received. To address this problem, several units have been able to effectively exploit their own mentorship networks, which span the Afghan unit's chains of command—i.e., contacting a mentor at a higher level who then ensures the request reaches his counterpart. This helps build local SOF capacity while still maintaining logistic support to operational units.

Assign senior and experienced individuals to key mentorship positions. Effective mentorship often requires assigning appropriately experienced individuals to key mentorship positions. This can require careful and creative personnel assignment that is not within established doctrine. For example, effective mentoring of an Afghan SOF battalion commander or equivalent may require the assignment of a field grade international officer, rather than a company grade officer. Alternatively, senior warrant officers might be used.

Maintain effective continuity across rotations. Continuity is critical to partner-force success. Often, the risk is that new units enter Afghanistan seeking to forgo the practices of prior units and instead forge ahead with new partnering practices and approaches identified during the pre-mission training period. Five practices can be adopted to ensure continuity:

1. Commands should establish a rotation cycle that returns teams to previously mentored units.
2. Staggered rotations, with commanders arriving several weeks to a month before the main element of the unit, can improve continuity.
3. Incoming teams must have a robust mechanism for procuring information on operations, the partner force, and partnership approaches from their predecessor units.
4. Higher-echelon units should provide oversight to identify best practices for continuity that can be applied across all SOF units.
5. Shared assessments maintained across echelons enhance awareness of partner capability for recently deployed units.

Pre-mission training (PMT) should include a mock partner force. PMT that is focused on preparation for the partnering mission appears limited in scope. In only a few cases did training focus on developing mentorship capability. In such cases, the primary approach was for mentor SOF units to train conventional force infantrymen and was deemed highly effective in preparing the unit for mentoring Afghan SOF.

Lessons for SOF Partnerships Beyond Afghanistan

Building partner capacity almost inevitability takes longer than anticipated. This seems to be true whether the host nation is weak and international SOF are committed in large numbers (Iraq, Afghanistan) or the host nation is relatively strong and international SOF are committed in small numbers (Colombia). Expectations should therefore be tempered for how quickly SOF partner units will develop.

Building partner-force "tooth" (operational combat units) much faster than "tail" (combat support and enablers) generates short-term gain but long-term pain. U.S. assets are typically used to provide tail functions in the near term while partner units get into the fight quickly, with the idea that those capabilities will be built later. Yet, as a result, these capabilities end up being anemic for a long time and perhaps never develop. This often means that capable partner SOF units underperform after U.S. forces are reduced. It would therefore seem to be better to emphasize building these capabilities earlier, accepting that this will reduce the speed of "tooth" development.

It may be worthwhile to explore nontraditional or atypical assignment patterns and durations for U.S. SOF personnel in these missions. Building partner capacity requires such extensive rapport development that personnel continuity is a paramount concern. Models other than the standard short deployment may be more effective. Just as one example, the British Army has long seconded officers to certain Gulf States to help build capacity. These officers, typically senior field grades near the end of their careers, are seconded for long accompanied tours, usually four years. While such an approach might not be suitable for host nations experiencing high levels of violence, it might be a much better use for many senior field grade SOF officers than a final tour as a Pentagon action officer.

Acknowledgments

The authors gratefully acknowledge the assistance of all special operations personnel who agreed to be interviewed for this report. In addition, we specially thank our colleagues Philip Padilla, Gillian Oak, and Jess Saunders for their hard work in helping facilitate research in Afghanistan. Francisco Walters provided critical administrative support to all facets of this study. In addition, James Torr provided needed editorial review on this manuscript. Colonel (ret.) David Maxwell of Georgetown University and Jefferson Marquis of RAND provided thoughtful and comprehensive reviews. Finally, we are especially grateful for the support of this study's sponsor, the NATO Special Operations Component Command–Afghanistan/Special Operations Joint Task Force–Afghanistan.

Abbreviations

AFB	Air Force base
ANA	Afghan National Army
ANASF	Afghan National Army Special Forces
ANASOC	Afghan National Army Special Operations Command
ANSF	Afghan National Security Forces
AOB	Advanced Operational Base
ATF	Afghan territorial force
AUC	Autodefensas Unidas de Colombia (United Self-Defense Forces of Colombia)
CF	commando force (Afghanistan)
CJSOTF-A	Combined Joint Special Operations Task Force–Afghanistan
CPA	Coalition Provisional Authority (Iraq)
CRU	Crisis Response Unit (Afghanistan)
CTC	Counter-Terrorism Command (Iraq)
CTS	Counter-Terrorism Service (Iraq)
ELN	Ejército de Liberación Nacional (National Liberation Army; Colombia)

FARC	Fuerzas Armadas Revolucionias de Colombia (Revolutionary Armed Forces of Colombia)
FID	foreign internal defense
GAULA	Grupos de Acción Unificada Libertad Personal (Unified Action Groups for Personal Liberty)
GDPSU	General Directorate of Police Special Units (Afghanistan)
ICTF	Iraqi Counterterrorism Task Force
ISAF	International Security Assistance Force
ISOF	Iraqi Special Operations Forces
ISR	intelligence, surveillance, and reconnaissance
JCET	Joint Combined Exchange for Training
LTT	Logistics Training Team
MEDEVAC	medical evacuation
MOD	Ministry of Defense
MOI	Ministry of Interior
NCO	noncommissioned officer
NDS	National Directorate of Security (Afghanistan)
NMU	national mission unit (Afghanistan)
NTEC	Network Targeting and Exploitation Center (Afghanistan)
OCINC	Office of the Commander in Chief (Iraq)
ODA	operational detachment–Alpha
OPTEMPO	operational tempo
PCOP	provincial chief of police (Afghanistan)

PDSS	pre-deployment site survey
PMT	pre-mission training
PRC	provincial response company (Afghanistan)
RIP	relief in place
SFG	Special Forces Group
SIGINT	signals intelligence
SOF	special operations forces
SOJTF-A	Special Operations Joint Task Force–Afghanistan
SOK	special operations *kandak* (Afghanistan)
SOTU	special operations task unit
UAV	unmanned aerial vehicle
VSO	village stability operations
WOLA	Washington Office on Latin America

CHAPTER ONE

Introduction

Over 13 years of war in Afghanistan, the United States has sought to develop a sustainable Afghan security structure. A critical ingredient to this effort has been the development and training of Afghan special operations forces (SOF). Numerous U.S. and international forces have played a critical role in Afghan SOF development. Some may continue to do so even after the conclusion of the International Security Assistance Force (ISAF) mission at the end of 2014. While U.S. SOF, including U.S. Army Special Forces, U.S. Navy SEALs, and U.S. Marine Corps Special Operations Teams, have focused on building up the Afghan Commandos and Special Forces, forces from the United Kingdom, Norway, Australia, and a host of other nations have worked to enhance the capability of Afghan special police outfits, including the Afghan Ministry of Interior's (MOI's) national mission units (NMUs) and provincial response companies (PRCs).

This coalition of units has undertaken various approaches to building Afghan SOF and so offers a host of best practices that can inform a broader understanding of how best to build the SOF capabilities of host-nation partners. "Building partner capacity" is a major strategic objective of current U.S. Special Operations Command commander ADM William McRaven.[1] Yet building this capacity will

---

[1] See Tyrone Marshall, "Building Allied Capability, Capacity Best Approach, McRaven Says," *American Forces Press Service*, April 9, 2013.

often be challenging, as efforts to build partner capacity in Mali have demonstrated.[2]

Consequently, this report seeks to cull the best practices in building partner capacity from a range of international units serving in Afghanistan. It accordingly draws on more than 80 interviews conducted in Afghanistan with representatives of seven contributing nations to ISAF.[3] It also draws lessons learned from U.S. SOF partner capacity building efforts in Iraq and Colombia. The goal is to identify both challenges and best practices for developing and utilizing SOF partnerships. The results are intended to inform continued SOF partnership efforts in Afghanistan after 2014 and beyond.

The report contains six main chapters. Chapters Two through Four summarize the results of battlefield circulations conducted in Afghanistan in the spring of 2013. RAND analysts conducted interviews with U.S. and coalition mentors at the MOI's NMUs and PRCs. Both of these unit types are tasked with conducting high-risk arrest operations and are mentored by a variety of coalition nations under the auspices of ISAF SOF. RAND analysts also visited three Commando special operations *kandaks* (SOKs), which are overseen by the Ministry of Defense's (MOD's) Afghan National Army Special Operations Command (ANASOC). The Commandos are light-infantry units akin to the U.S. Army Rangers and are mentored by U.S. special operations teams under the auspices of the Combined Joint Special Operations Task Force–Afghanistan (CJSOTF-A). Both ISAF SOF and CJSOTF-A are subordinate commands of the Special Operations Joint Task Force–Afghanistan (SOJTF-A), which sponsored this study. Chapter Two focuses on the MOI NMUs, Chapter Three on the MOI PRCs, and Chapter Four on the ANASOC Commandos. Analyses are based on interviews with a wide cross section of coalition partners,

---

[2]   See Adam Nossiter, Eric Schmitt, and Mark Mazetti, "French Strikes in Mali Supplant Caution of U.S.," *New York Times*, January 13, 2013; and Michael R. Noggle "Senegalese and Malian Soldiers Train with U.S. Special Forces in Mali," Special Operations Task Force-103 Public Affairs press release, May 17, 2010.

[3]   The primary interview protocol can be found in the Appendix.

including American, British, Norwegian, Australian, Lithuanian, and Romanian forces.

In addition, RAND examined two additional case studies of SOF partnership efforts. Chapter Five reviews U.S. efforts to build and mentor the Iraqi Special Operations Forces (ISOF) from 2003 to 2012, and Chapter Six reviews U.S. assistance to Colombian SOF that began in earnest in the late 1990s and continues to the present. The Iraq case study was chosen as it represents efforts to build, from the ground up, an indigenous SOF capacity. In contrast, the Colombian case study represents an enduring SOF partnership effort that managed to help foster a relatively professional and capable special operations force. Analyses for both case studies were supported by interviews with U.S. Navy SEAL operators as well as representatives of 5th and 10th Special Forces Groups (SFGs; Iraq case study) and 7th SFG (Colombian case study). These empirical sections provide the basis for Chapter Seven, in which we present a set of best practices as well as potential means to mitigate challenges.

Before proceeding, a brief definition of the term *partnership* in the context of this report is needed. In the past decade, the term *partner* has come into wide use in the Department of Defense, but the only doctrinal definitions for the term are vague and/or generic. Essentially any entity that works with the United States can doctrinally be called "partner."[4]

While providing a universally acceptable doctrinal definition is beyond the scope of this report, it is important that the Defense Department develop a clearer definition of *partnership*. The definition used in this report is a potential starting point, as it provides a more specific meaning for the term. We define *partnership* as a habitual relationship between a special operations unit (or units) from a host nation

---

[4] See, for example, Joint Publication 1-02, *Department of Defense Dictionary of Military and Associated Terms*, Washington, D.C.: U.S. Department of Defense, November 8, 2010 (as amended through July 16, 2014); and Joint Publication 3-22, *Foreign Internal Defense*, Washington, D.C.: U.S. Department of Defense, July 12, 2010. For more extensive discussion of these issues, see Christopher Paul, Colin P. Clarke, Beth Grill, Stephanie Young, Jennifer D. P. Moroney, Joe Hogler, and Christine Leah, *What Works Best When Building Partner Capacity and Under What Circumstances?* Santa Monica, Calif.: RAND Corporation, MG-1253/1-OSD, 2013, pp. 7–9.

and an external special operations unit (or units) not indigenous to the host nation. This habitual relationship involves extensive training and advising conducted in the host nation by the nonindigenous unit or units. The examples of partnership explored in this report are all in the context of an internal war in the host nation and so are partnerships in support of foreign internal defense (FID), but this need not be the case in all special operations partnerships.

For this definition of *partnership*, there is no specific ratio of host-nation to external SOF in any combat operations. However, a partner unit is not just a surrogate or proxy force that merely provides placement and access for the external SOF. Partnership requires that the host-nation SOF have an independent institutional existence and that there be some effort to build the capacity of these forces for independent activity without the external SOF partner.[5]

It is also important at this point to clarify a recurring theme in this report: the tension between achieving immediate operational effects and developing enduring partner capacity. *Immediate operational effects* are defined as the tangible results of operations undertaken by the international forces and host-nation SOF units in partnership (e.g., militants killed or captured as a result of a raid). *Enduring partner capacity* is defined as the ability of the host-nation SOF unit to conduct certain operations absent international support (e.g., to plan raids).

Achieving immediate operational effects and developing enduring partner capacity are not automatically and inherently in tension. As the examples suggest, a raid that is planned and conducted primarily by host-nation SOF with only modest support from international forces achieves both. However, in Afghanistan and Iraq, tension between the two arose as the demand for immediate operational effects vastly surpassed the ability of host-nation SOF, absent extensive support from international forces.

The result has been a situation where international forces provide much of the intelligence, planning, and logistical support to enable

---

[5] For more discussion of partners versus surrogate/proxy forces, see Austin Long, "Partners or Proxies? U.S. and Host Nation Cooperation in Counterterrorism Operations," *CTC Sentinel*, November 30, 2011.

host-nation SOF to achieve immediate operational effects. This has the effect of stunting the development of a host-nation ability to develop and utilize intelligence, to plan, and to provide logistical support. Continuing the example of raids, if a host-nation unit can hypothetically develop, plan, and support one raid per night but the demand from higher headquarters calls for three per night, the international mentor unit must take over much of these functions, limiting the development of host-nation capacity at anything other than the tactical level.

In interviews over the summer of 2013, some members of the special operations community in Afghanistan described this tension by drawing an analogy to weight lifting. All things being equal, another repetition of a given weight will lead to more muscle development. If a small amount of outside assistance in lifting the weight can help an individual perform more repetitions, then muscle development will be enhanced. However, if that outside assistance begins to exceed the amount of effort expended by the individual performing the repetitions, then muscle development will be decreased, and may even atrophy.

The same pattern applies to SOF partnership if one substitutes immediate operational effects for repetitions and partner capacity for muscle development. If host-nation SOF are performing most of the work needed to create immediate operational effects, from planning and resourcing to conducting the operation, then there is no tension between immediate operational effects and building capacity. Indeed, if international forces can provide just enough support to push the host-nation SOF to their limits in terms of creating immediate operational effects, this may actually enhance both effects and partner capacity.

However, if the demand for immediate operational effects is much greater than the current capacity of host-nation SOF, then international forces will inevitably end up providing so much assistance that the ability of supported host-nation forces will not progress and may atrophy. The critical point is to find the appropriate balance, which must be clearly agreed on throughout the chain of command. Lack of clarity about this balance can produce misunderstandings between higher headquarters and those units actually partnering with host-nation SOF.

CHAPTER TWO

SOF Partnership in Afghanistan: The Ministry of Interior's National Mission Units

The NMUs and PRCs conduct high-risk arrest, counterterrorism, and counternarcotic missions under the auspices of the Afghan MOI. The General Directorate of Police Special Units (GDPSU), a major directorate under the deputy minister of interior for security, commands and controls the NMUs and PRCs. ISAF SOF, a subordinate command of SOJTF-A, is a multinational command that will provide direct mentorship to GDPSU, the NMUs, and PRCs through the end of 2014. This chapter focuses on the NMUs, while the next chapter addresses PRCs.

The NMUs are among the best-performing Afghan National Security Forces (ANSF) units, in part because they are among the oldest units in the Afghan SOF community and have been shielded from many of the effects of poor Afghan governance by partner forces that have worked with them consistently over time. GDPSU has three NMUs, which are Afghan tier-one units. The three NMUs are Afghan Territorial Force (ATF) 444, based in Helmand; Commando Force (CF) 333 in Logar; and the Crisis Response Unit (CRU, sometimes called Task Force 222) in Kabul. The CRU has responsibility for security in Kabul and is the first responder to high-profile attacks that threaten the capital. The other two NMUs cover a broader geographic area and conduct a variety of reconnaissance and high-risk arrest operations. Each NMU has four squadrons, each consisting of three operational platoons. CF 333 and ATF 444 are partnered with British forces, while the CRU is partnered with Norwegian special operators.

Methodology

During field research in Afghanistan, RAND visited the GDPSU headquarters in Kabul (partnered with ISAF SOF mentors), ATF 444 and CF 333 (partnered with British forces), and the CRU (partnered with Norwegian SOF). Interviews were conducted with both international mentors and Afghan officers and enlisted personnel.

Partnership Approach

Task Organization

The mentor units of the NMUs employed a variety of task organizations to manage the mentoring mission. In the case of Norwegian and some British forces, there were designated lead mentors for each squadron. For British forces mentoring CF 333, color sergeants (E7/OR-7 in U.S./NATO ranking systems) served as primary mentors to the individual squadrons. They helped supervise training, participated in joint operations, and advised Afghans on how the NMUs could conduct unilateral operations. Their goal was to ensure that each squad had one "go-to person" and to support relationship building.[1] These mentors collectively felt that the color sergeant was the appropriate rank for the squadron mentors because they generally had between 12 and 15 years in service, much of it running training for their home units.[2] Similarly, the Norwegians assigned one SOF team to mentor each squadron across the operational and training cycles.[3] While this maintained a consistent mentor-partner force relationship, it was more broad based in that the entire team played a role in mentoring its counterparts.

---

[1]   Senior officer, mentor force, March 1, 2013.

[2]   Senior noncommissioned officer (NCO), mentor force, March 1, 2013.

[3]   ANSF operate on what are referred to as green, amber, and red cycles. The green cycle refers to the time the unit is dedicated to operations, the amber cycle refers to the time the unit is dedicated to training, and the red cycle refers to time spent on leave. A typical battalion-sized formation will generally have three operational companies. The companies will have staggered green, amber, and red cycles.

By contrast, British forces mentoring ATF 444 had a much more expansive view of the mentoring relationship, arguing that "every man is a mentor," even the motor pool sergeant.[4] While corporals did serve as counterparts to Afghan captains, and sergeants to first sergeants, they were not the sole parties responsible for managing the relationships with Afghan partner units.

Mission Focus

Norwegian and some British forces described early mentoring partnerships in which the goal was either to put an "Afghan face" onto essentially unilateral coalition operations or gradually bring Afghan units up to speed through partnering on advanced ISAF operations. As one officer commented, "We have been training for nine years, but we have not been mentoring. . . . With training you are directing them and not giving them ownership, while mentoring is empowering."[5] One veteran of many deployments counted this as his single biggest lesson learned; if he could rewind the clock, "I would put much more focus on mentoring of [the Afghan force] early. At that time, we had the mission to take care of security in Kabul and we were getting bad guys [and] bringing the [Afghan force] with us. We were 50-percent partnering and 50-percent operations."[6] By contrast, mentors at ATF 444 still viewed operations as a key part of its mission, as it has force-protection responsibilities for the British task force, but the mentors reported that the balance is changing.

Recently, however, these units have placed greater emphasis on mentoring Afghan operational capability, even if that means sacrificing some degree of operational effects on the insurgency.[7] One British mentor for CF 333 encapsulated this by asserting that they now "operate to transition" by focusing on training and mentorship rather than "transition to operate" or simply look for an Afghan face for operations.

---

[4]   Senior officer, mentor force, March 5, 2013.

[5]   Senior officer, mentor force, March 1, 2013.

[6]   Senior officer, mentor force, February 26, 2013.

[7]   Senior officer, mentor force, February 26, 2013.

Likewise, the Norwegians partnering with CRU reported that they are less concerned with racking up operational statistics, such as detainees captured, than with helping Afghans achieve effective capabilities to plan and conduct their own missions. The metric for this would be the level of support the Norwegians must provide to enable CRU missions, rather than the number of missions.

One key aspect of operating "to transition" is allowing partner units the opportunity to fail. Contrasting his approach to those mentors who "are telling their guys every little detail," one Norwegian officer argues, "It is counterproductive to do it for them. We don't care how [they] do it as long as [they] fix the problem. Sometimes I have [mentors] who can do something in a quicker and smoother manner than [Afghan] guys, but . . . I'm not interested in how they can do it."[8] As one senior Afghan CRU officer noted, the difference between Norwegian mentors and others he has worked with is that Norwegian SOF "will let you drop, drop, drop, drop and you are about to drown and they will then pick you up."[9] Such a "tough love" approach has shown results: "While they saw us drop, they also saw us stand up."[10]

Operating to transition also means promoting independent operations. NMU mentors, especially at CF 333 and CRU, for example, attempted to limit the number of coalition mentors on Afghan missions. A number of Afghan missions were unilateral and conducted with no direct coalition support, while for others the ratio of foreign to host-nation forces was as low as three to five international personnel partnered with an assault force, with several more possibly embedded with fires support or cordon forces. This compared to Afghan National Army (ANA) Commando *kandaks* that, until 2013, typically went on operations with a full U.S. SOF team of 12 to 16 members.

Mentor forces also provided "secret overwatch" by covertly placing international forces on standby near the objective. This allowed the Afghan forces to behave truly independently, not knowing there was a safety net for Afghan and foreign forces should the operation go awry.

---

8   Senior officer, mentor force, February 26, 2013.

9   Afghan officer, February 26, 2013.

10   Afghan officer, February 26, 2013.

The footprint for these mentor forces was light and becoming lighter, with one unit indicating plans to reduce its size by two-thirds in the next three rotations. At the time of this writing, the unit has manpower to assist with two operations, "but soon it will only be one and finally they will have too few to do operations."[11]

The NMU mentors also pushed for greater reliance on Afghan intelligence. The British forces mentoring CF 333 strove to provide Afghans only with those intelligence feeds that will be available to them post-withdrawal. For example, without knowing whether the Afghans will receive unmanned aerial vehicles (UAVs), they did not provide UAV feeds to the Afghans. Withholding assets can at times seem cruel, but the resulting capabilities are more sustainable; as one Afghan officer said, "It doesn't need a technological solution but it has to work."[12]

One challenge of promoting independent operational capability is that coalition personnel miss out on operations. As one mentor commented, "It's frustrating for a lot of guys not to go out as much, especially the younger ones. But generally there is an understanding that it's for the collective good. Leadership is important in setting expectations and in expectation management."[13]

While much of the data on NMU operations are classified, some unclassified observations are possible. One is that the effort to force NMUs to rely more on Afghan intelligence and to plan their own operations has significantly but not catastrophically decreased operational tempo (OPTEMPO). Another is that intelligence sharing between NMUs and certain other elements of the Afghan government has improved in some cases and, more importantly, the relationship is beginning to become institutionalized rather than based purely on personal relationships (though personal relationships remained central through 2013).[14]

---

[11] Senior NCO, mentor force, March 1, 2013.

[12] Afghan officer, February 26, 2013.

[13] NCO, mentor force, March 1, 2013.

[14] Based on observations through August 2013.

Rapport

Building rapport between host-nation and partner units is key to successful mentoring and partnering. Norwegian SOF, for example, focused on building friendships, playing sports together, and even engaging in Afghan dance and traditional activities. Among the British forces, while friendship and personal relationships were important, one color sergeant indicated that he built senior professional relationships first, in deference to the Afghan command hierarchy: "Now that I don't teach officers much, I can build relationships with the men. It doesn't threaten their command structure."[15] For each unit, building religious and cultural understanding was key. As one Afghan officer of CF 333 said of his mentors' rapport-building efforts, "I can't see how it would be better. The British invited the Afghans here for Christmas dinner. We invited them for Eid."[16]

Physical base layout and security posture also affect rapport. At one installation, the mentor force had a separate living compound and tactical operations center. However, these were located within the Afghan base and were adjacent to the Afghan headquarters, mess hall, and unit barracks. Officers and enlisted personnel from the mentor force walked freely through the Afghan sections of the base. At CRU, RAND analysts visited the standby CRU squadron located in Kabul. There, the Norwegian mentor team built a small and relatively unsecured enclave inside the larger CRU facility. The enclave was adjacent to the CRU's living quarters and allowed unfettered interaction between the mentors and the CRU operators.[17]

In addition, security posture plays a key role in rapport building. Some NMU mentors made it a point to note that they seldom wear more than pistols when working with Afghan soldiers, and at times were completely unarmed while in Afghan areas of the base. Afghans

---

[15] NCO, mentor force, March 2, 2013.

[16] Afghan officer, March 2, 2013.

[17] The Norwegian SOF headquarters is located on a large ISAF military base to facilitate coordination with ISAF components and the Norwegian national element, but it is not co-located with any CRU counterpart organization. The main body of Norwegian SOF is co-located with CRU and built as a small enclave inside the larger CRU facility.

appreciate this as a sign of trust, saying, "[a] good thing in the mentor relationship is how close the mentors are to us. They will go out to the range without a weapon."[18] Being unarmed or lightly armed is both a sign of trust and the product of a long, trusting relationship. As one interviewee said, "Our concern isn't protecting ourselves from green-on-blue; it's not an issue. That's because there is an enduring relationship with guys coming back year after year."[19] (Continuity of personnel will be dealt with at greater length later in this chapter.)

Finally, it is noteworthy that British forces made a concerted effort to educate key Afghan commanders at the Royal Military Academy Sandhurst. Several recent commanders from CF 333 were sent to the Great Britain for formal military education, as was the CRU commander. These commanders exhibited high pride in their British education, with one commander making a point to show visiting RAND analysts his Sandhurst graduation photos. By and large, this education seemed to help these commanders improve their English-language skills as well as enhance their understanding of British military tactics.

Key Tasks
Weaning from Unsustainable Foreign Inputs
Some Afghan SOF units have been successful in part due to the special assistance mentors have provided to them. Most significantly, top-up pay was provided to some police officers—incentive payments that totaled four to six times what soldiers make through their regular salaries. This affected the individual careers of soldiers as well as the dissemination of skills across the total force, because "going into the mainstream carries a financial penalty and presently there is no career movement [within the unit hierarchy]."[20] In the longer term, the salary was far higher than anything the Afghan government could sustain on its own, and many mentors felt that the soldiers receiving top-up pay would not continue to serve when their financial incentive disappears. In a worst-case scenario, these well-trained forces "will have to find

---

[18] Afghan officer, March 2, 2013.

[19] Senior NCO, mentor force, February 26, 2013.

[20] Senior officer, mentor force, March 5, 2013.

other wells to drink from," potentially bringing other subnational or international payers into the picture.[21]

On balance, was the top-up pay a good idea? Some respondents felt that, for all its flaws, it was necessary: "At the end of the day, we had to raise a force, and top-up pay was how. We were able to be more selective—got great recruits with college degrees."[22] However, other police officers were not given top-up pay, and it was difficult to discern from the interviews a significant difference in retention rates between the different units. Specific retention rates between these units were not reviewed as part of this report. It is also unclear whether soldiers receiving top-up pay necessarily outperform those who do not receive outside incentives.

In addition to top-up pay, some mentors provided a high degree of financial support for supplies and maintenance. In one location, for example, mentors have taken responsibility for upkeep of Afghan areas of the camp, spending thousands of dollars per month in the process. Afghan NMUs faced challenges common to the rest of the Afghan forces in terms of corruption and malign political influence, and because of these, when mentors attempt to remove themselves from this process, the base falls into disrepair until they step back in. Mentor units have begun to employ similar weaning, or "tough love," strategies to promote Afghan sustainability, the results of which had not matured in late 2013.

Comprehensive Mentoring

Where a partner unit is unable to accomplish its objective on its own— for example, requiring aviation support or supplies—requests often stall. Mentors often described this as "the system," noting that their capable units encountered roadblocks every time they dealt with the rest of the Afghan system. Mentors dealt with these roadblocks in different ways. One best practice was to engage in what one respondent called "comprehensive mentoring," saying, "I want to see how [the part-

---

[21] NCO, mentor force, March 2, 2013.

[22] NCO, mentor force, March 2, 2013.

ner unit] works within the GDPSU system . . . so I care about things that are out of my [partner] unit; I care about the system around it."[23]

To help his partner unit work within the system, the mentor worked with external mentors whose partner units had relationships with his partner unit. For example, when an Afghan supply officer submitted a request form to GDPSU, the mentor would call the GDPSU supply officer's mentor to make sure he knew the request has been submitted. This allowed the GDSPU's supply officer the opportunity to receive direct mentorship on provisioning the supplies. Where mentors did not use comprehensive mentoring, they sometimes sent these requests to their national military element at their home country's embassy. While this does draw attention to unmet needs, it seems not to be as efficient as the informal building of relationships with fellow mentors. The ability to engage in comprehensive mentoring was limited by geography, though, and mentors in remote areas may have found it difficult to identify and engage their peers.

Comprehensive mentoring also included developing NMU capacity to coordinate and orchestrate the full set of tactical units and enablers. The British forces mentoring CF 333 effectively used a table-top exercise to help train Afghan planning capability. CF 333 mentors specifically developed a tabletop exercise to help commanders think through alternative medical evacuation (MEDEVAC) options. Bringing together the operations officer, signals officers, and medics, they helped the operations officer realize that if he delegates MEDEVAC tasks to subordinates, they will be able to accomplish more themselves without relying on ISAF. Thus, an important lesson was learned, not only about MEDEVAC but about command guidance and working independently.

Intelligence and Warrant-Based Operations

One key sign of a unit's sustainability is its ability to identify and pursue its own targets. This requires both an intelligence capability and a commitment to warrant-based operations. Where units are pursuing targets provided by ISAF intelligence, they are often not told

---

[23] Senior officer, mentor force, February 26, 2013.

the location or identity of the target because of restrictions on sharing this information. This diminishes their role in planning and executing operations, and it sets a precedent for bypassing Afghan rule of law, which specifies that warrants are necessary for law enforcement officers to pursue Afghan citizens. That said, NMUs vary somewhat in the extent to which they pull intelligence in from Afghan sources.

The primary source for Afghan intelligence should be the Network Targeting and Exploitation Center (NTEC), an MOI intelligence fusion center in Kabul, but NTEC is a young organization and its ability to produce intelligence varies according to location. At CRU, intelligence comes both from NTEC and ISAF, but this has been identified as an area to transition more completely to the CRU. In the months preceding the RAND visit in March 2013, CF 333 transitioned completely to an Afghan-led, warrant-based operations model. British mentors help to facilitate fusion between CF 333's internal intelligence staff and the broader Afghan intelligence community, which includes NTEC, the National Directorate of Security (NDS), and others. In 2013, the CF 333 intelligence cycle was a frontrunner among Afghan units, with a battle rhythm that included weekly targeting meetings with GDPSU, NDS, and NTEC, and required these units to provide information that is complete enough to be the basis for Afghan warrants.

Evaluation

Mentor units employed various means to evaluate the success of partner programs and their own work. Norwegian SOF maintained a milestone plan that charted goals for the CRU against actual progress. British forces used a more elaborate system, called *performance profiling*, successfully pioneered by the Royal Marines. In this system, each Afghan staff directorate that is charged with overseeing personnel (referred to as S-1), intelligence (S-2), operations (S-3), logistics (S-4), plans (S-5), or communications (S-6) in CF 333 was evaluated on key performance tasks along an 8-point scale. The tasks and responsibilities for each section were broken down into their key constituent parts. For example, the CF 333 S-2 was assessed, in part, along the following lines:

Integrates with Afghan J-2 structure and effectively obtains intelligence from them; . . . Identifies and articulates intelligence requirements, particularly for force protection purposes; Conducts information management; Analyses and assesses intelligence; Evidential exploitation; Processes detainees; etc.[24]

This review practice was unique in that goals and progress were judged by mutual agreement between mentor and partner forces. Each conducted a separate evaluation of the unit's progress, and the resulting ratings were decided between them. This ensured that the criteria by which the mentors judged success were known to the partner force, and assessments were either agreed on or at least understood by Afghan officers. It also provided an opportunity for the British to mentor the Afghans on performance assessments.

Continuity and Pre-Mission Training

Continuity

One of the key aspects of the NMU mentor units that set them apart from other mentoring and partnering forces was the rotation pattern of the force. In the case of British forces, for example, there was a commitment to send the same units back to work with the partner force, which meant that most mentors had completed three to four rotations with the same Afghan unit. Norwegian SOF also relied on repeat tours to CRU. This created a deep level of familiarity with the partner unit and allowed the mentor force to use short rotations without losing institutional knowledge. For one commander, this allowed him to more seamlessly "tweak" the mission when mentors got too entrenched in habits: "They get shaken out of their old pattern and then pick back up again at a more advanced place."[25]

---

[24] Senior officer, mentor force, March 1, 2013.

[25] Senior officer, mentor force, February 26, 2013.

Seeing "familiar faces" also led to trust-based relationships, as opposed to transactional ones.[26] One Afghan officer noted that repeat rotations helped mentors understand how the Afghans progressed to their current level, and "if someone with no experience comes back we say, 'We have ten years experience, who are you?'"[27] However, another Afghan officer emphasized that the mission would continue even without those relationships, saying, "It's nice to have our friends come back, of course. [But] we have to—us as the receiving support unit—say 'sure.' If you are starving and somebody hands you a hamburger one day and a pizza the next, you won't say no."[28]

Another key piece of NMU mentor units' continuity plan was the relief in place/transfer of authority (RIP/TOA, often simply referred to as RIP). All NMU mentor units employed a staggered RIP, with commanders arriving several weeks to a month before the main element of the unit. While actual overlap in theater may only be a week, incoming units conducted predeployment trips, sending elements to gather the latest information on the campaign. However, because of the small size of the home units, rotating forces knew each other well already—for example, a British commander mentoring CF 333 had known his replacement for 15 years. This led to a high level of communication between rotating units. For example, as one mentor force officer observed, "We have a weekly [videoteleconference] and [the incoming personnel] read all the [situation reports]." The incoming and outgoing units also share frequent phone calls to discuss new and ongoing topics.[29] Another commander noted, "They start RIP-ing from the time before they deploy, as they are already in touch with predecessors before they leave [home country] for the mission."[30]

Finally, the British ensured continuity through a robust policy- and guidance-setting process, with a single headquarters providing

---

[26] Afghan officer, February 26, 2013.

[27] Afghan officer, March 2, 2013.

[28] Afghan officer, February 26, 2013.

[29] Senior officer, mentor force, February 26, 2013.

[30] Senior NCO, mentor force, March 1, 2013.

command guidance for all British NMU mentor units. This allowed the British to maintain best practices across rotations. As one officer described it, "You got to have the continuity. [The] American structure does not have that pillar of direction. [The] U.S. is more tempo- and operational statistics–focused, but that is not what we are about. We are a small . . . organization. We get clear direction from our command on how to do operations."[31] When asked, mentor units felt that their higher echelons generally provided the right level of command guidance, neither too detailed nor too vague.

Where the headquarters provided guidance as to what worked and what did not, specific policy was set at the level of the overall British task force in theater, yet this remains a lower echelon–driven process. When units try something that works well, the task force "will write it into policy and it goes to [the British task force] to be approved and made the official way that the mission is done. It usually happens once per rotation or so."[32] Although Norwegian SOF does not have a similar written policy, it does have a milestone plan for evaluation that fills a similar purpose. That document was modified but maintained across rotations. It looks forward two to three years and was a tool for discussion between rotating units throughout the tour, as it was reevaluated every three months.

Pre-Mission Training

While pre-mission training (PMT) played a role in NMU mentors' continuity, it may not have played as great a role as it did in other units, because these units relied more heavily on other forms of continuity (such as repeat rotations). In the case of British forces partnered with CF 333, because the mission has endured over nine years, most PMT focused on "general operations" or small-unit tactics rehearsal rather than FID-specific training. Furthermore, NCOs on the mentor force already benefited from mentoring courses required to become an NCO.[33] Another respondent disliked the PMT, noting that it was

---

[31] Senior officer, mentor force, March 1, 2013.

[32] Enlisted, mentor force, March 1, 2013.

[33] NCO, mentor force, March 1, 2013.

more appropriate for the days when the unit conducted primarily uni-lateral, offensive operations. He suggested, "Any training is best done here mentoring the Afghans and working with the units. Better to send guys here for pre-deployment training during the recce."[34] Generally, respondents felt that their previous rotations and more-general career training and mentoring expertise were most relevant to their success in this mission.

Summary

In summary, the NMUs, consisting of CF 333, ATF 444, and CRU, were among the highest-performing Afghan special operations units as of the end of 2013. These units, especially CF 333 and CRU, were increasingly conducting unilateral operations. Even partnered missions were conducted with a shrinking number of coalition personnel. Intelligence-operations integration was especially strong, with mentors at CF 333 shaping relatively advanced connections between CF 333 operators and intelligence channels at NTEC and NDS.

The advances across these units were aided by a number of sound partnership approaches. NMU mentors focused on building Afghan capacity rather than focusing solely on achieving operational effects. They sought to wean coalition support to operations by curtailing the number of coalition personnel on Afghan missions and limiting certain levels of intelligence enablers to foster a sustainable Afghan approach to operations. Rapport and continuity were especially strong areas of mentorship, with British and Norwegian troops performing numer-ous repeat tours with their Afghan partners. Such repeat tours played an especially important dividend in building strong relationships with Afghan personnel.

---

[34] NCO, mentor force, March 2, 2013. *Recce* in this context is what U.S. SOF would refer to as a pre-deployment site survey (PDSS), a visit to a unit/site before deployment to develop an understanding of the environment.

CHAPTER THREE

SOF Partnership in Afghanistan: The Ministry of Interior's Provincial Response Companies

In addition to the three NMUs, GDPSU had 19 PRCs across Afghanistan at the time of this assessment. PRCs are based at the provincial level and are directly overseen by the individual provincial chiefs of police (PCOPs). PRCs are intended to conduct provincial-level special police operations to counter terrorism and narcotics and support operations against criminal groups.[1] Each PRC is generally composed of three platoons. Each platoon is composed of three eight-person squads, a sniper team, an explosive ordinance disposal team, and a sensitive site exploitation team. PRCs are typically smaller and less capable than NMUs. However, the wide geographic dispersal of PRCs and their provincial, rather than national or regional, focus make them a potentially important Afghan SOF capability. PRCs face a variety of challenges, many stemming from their provincial-level focus.

Methodology

The methodology for this chapter is the same as the previous chapter. In addition to interviews at GDPSU headquarters, RAND analysts visited PRCs in Kandahar (Lithuanian SOF), Uruzgan (Australian SOF), and Kapisa (joint U.S.-Romanian SOF). Interviews were conducted with both U.S. and coalition mentors, as well as select Afghan officers

---

[1] CDR Don Plummer, briefing to SOF Academic Week–OEF XXI, May 28–31, 2013.

and NCOs. These interviews are believed to be representative of most of the range of variation in capability across PRCs, but this chapter is nonetheless more tentative than the preceding chapter, as only four out of 19 PRCs are represented.

Partnership Approach

Task Organization

The task organization of PRC mentor units was similar to those partnered with NMUs, though this varied widely according to the size of the mentor force. For example, among the units visited, the Lithuanian task force, which mentored PRCs Kandahar and Zabul, had only about 60 people. This was small relative to the partner-force sizes, but personnel noted that, though the numbers are small, "SOF is [flexible]. We will do the mission with whatever we have. It's a short deployment: We can work overtime."[2] The Australians, who mentored the PRC in Uruzgan, had a dedicated special operations task group of more than 200 men that provided logistics and other services for the PRC, as well as an NDS unit.

At PRC Kapisa, there was one U.S. and two Romanian special operations task units (SOTUs; equivalent to operational detachment–Alpha [ODA] in NATO terms). These units fell under Combined Special Operations Task Force 10, which oversaw mentoring at seven PRCs. At each PRC there was a U.S. SOTU combined with an Eastern European SOTU. Contributing nations included Romania, Estonia, Hungary, and Slovakia. Task Force 10 represents a unique mission in Afghanistan, as it seeks to not only train and mentor Afghan PRC units but also enhance the SOF skills of the contributing Eastern European nations.

Mission Focus

PRC mentors reported tensions in the degree to which they should conduct operations to achieve battlespace effects versus focus on devel-

---

[2]   Junior officer, mentor force, March 3, 2013.

oping PRC capabilities. While mentor units themselves understood and appreciated the need to prioritize the training mission, absent clear guidance from higher headquarters directing them to do so, the focus defaulted to direct action. As one mentor said, "The missions continue to change. There is not a strong campaign plan of 'here is the goal and here is where you fit on the line.' So the problem with that is when I first got here I was told your job is to get [Joint Prioritized Engagement List targets]." This individual suggested that it would be better to instead "develop some lasting process, which is support for an anti-insurgency."[3]

Mentors at other PRCs report that a focus on operational effects may limit or even retard a unit's capacity for independent operations. One mentor observed that such operations "exceeded the absorptive capacity of the Afghans and thus unintentionally retarded improvement in many respects."[4] A mentor at a third PRC noted that while such operations gave Afghans a "wider range" of mission experiences and so enhanced their capabilities, such missions will be out of Afghan reach once the coalition withdraws. The mentor assessed that, after withdrawal, the Afghans "will merely roll down the road in trucks to look at checkpoints."[5]

At PRC Kapisa, the U.S. SOTU's goal was to mentor the Romanians, who in turn were to mentor the Afghans. Training was conducted through two four-man training cells, each composed of two Americans and two Romanians. The cells reportedly took turns every week on determining the training curriculum, but the precise training roles evolved by design over the course of the deployment. Initially, the U.S. team ran day-to-day training with Romanians in observation, but as Romanian skills evolved they began to take over the lion's share of the training responsibilities. It was the same with operations. As one U.S. NCO noted, "We had our first two patrols where Romanians are

---

3   Anonymous interview, date withheld.

4   Anonymous interview, date withheld.

5   Anonymous interview, date withheld.

running the patrols. . . . [The Romanians are both] running the patrol and planning the patrol. We are just out there for assistance."[6]

Rapport

Rapport between Afghans and ISAF SOF mentors appeared strong. The Lithuanian mentors' approach to mentoring was ingrained in troops by the command. For example, the mentors sent the PRC commander to Lithuania for treatment when he was injured by an improvised explosive device, which helped build rapport. These efforts are paired with a general philosophy of closeness: Lithuanian and Afghan forces have bonded through guard shifts and off-hours spent together engaging in sign language, football, and joking around with each other. One mentor noted that Lithuanians are comfortable doing things the Afghan way—"We act like brothers and hold hands"—and suggested further that Lithuania's status as a nation newly independent of occupying forces helps mentors to empathize with partner forces.[7]

At PRC Zabul, mentors found that the foundations of good rapport were "respect, interpersonal relationships, and repetition of tours—they are happy to see us again when we return."[8] At the Australian-mentored PRC, troops found that good rapport has tangible benefits, because "being a good friend can allow a mentor to push harder without causing offense."[9] They suggested that inviting partner forces to do something as a favor, rather than directing them to do it as part of their job, can be an effective technique for obtaining results without offending. Finally, rapport at PRC Kapisa has been aided by a strong commander's intent that set clear expectations for the combined U.S.-Romanian element. As one NCO reflected:

> [The team leader] has four rules. . . . You will treat all the Afghans with respect. You will not lay hands on them unless [in an] emer-

---

[6] NCO, mentor force, March 10, 2013.

[7] Officer, mentor forces, March 3, 2013.

[8] Junior officer, mentor force, March 3, 2013. RAND analysts did not visit PRC Zabul, but interviewed Lithuanian SOF who were mentoring the PRC while visiting PRC Kandahar.

[9] Officer, mentor force, March 2, 2013.

gency. You will reward them and congratulate them on things they do well. You will show them that you care. It rolls up to treating them with professional courtesy and treating them with respect.[10]

One test of the depth of rapport between partner and mentor is the process of weaning Afghan partner units off of logistics and supplies that have been provided by mentors for many years. The drawdown of troops puts mentors in the uncomfortable position of leaving Afghans to fend for themselves with a failing supply system: "I used to be able to buy and spend stuff and I can't do that. . . . Now I say I'm sorry you don't have blankets. It is not good for rapport but it works as a forcing function."[11] By late 2013 this tension was still ongoing, but clearer judgments about how well SOF partners have addressed this challenge will be possible after 2014.

Key Tasks
Logistics
In the past, PRC mentor forces tended to supply critical items themselves, in an attempt to shield the partner force from the effects of poor supply.[12] However, by 2013 the approach was to say "no" to logistics requests to build a self-sustaining capability within the PRC. This forced PRCs to learn to train and operate without logistical support from mentors.

However, coalition forces took an active approach to mentoring the Afghan logistics system. In an approach reminiscent of other Afghan SOF mentor units, the mentors at PRC Kapisa drew on a coalition network, including provincial government advisors who were called Provincial Augmentation Teams. When the Afghans submitted a logistics request up their channels, the mentors submitted the same request to the Provincial Augmentation Team, which could then

---

[10] Senior NCO, mentor force, March 10, 2013.

[11] Officer, mentor force, March 9, 2013.

[12] As one mentor suggested, the mission "would have been much more difficult to do relying on ISAF or Afghan logistics." Officer, mentor force, March 2, 2013.

mentor the Afghan headquarters to service the request. As one mentor put it, "This took us a decade to figure out. We find it gets lost on the Afghan side, but at each level there is a [mentor liaison officer]. . . . If it gets to the governor and they say we won't get that to you then there is CF presence [with the governor] who says they need it. . . . It is working but not very effective."[13]

Enablers and Sustainable Operations
A heavy reliance on coalition enablers risks a significant drop in PRC capabilities during transition. Mentors at PRC Kapisa, for example, noted that they were required to have a C-130 on station during operations and that they benefited from a host of intelligence, surveillance, and reconnaissance (ISR) assets. As one mentor noted, "The PRC will not have those capabilities." Like the British forces mentoring CF 333, PRC Kapisa's mentors do not share operational ISR assets with the Afghans. In the words of one mentor, "If they get addicted to that, then they would never cross the wadi."[14]

The Lithuanians, mentoring PRC Kandahar and PRC Zabul, also understood the importance of sustainability. Here, the task force urged its partner force to conduct mounted and dismounted patrols to reduce the reliance on rotary-wing lift assets. While this was working fairly well, it did reduce speed and mobility. In response, they were trying to link together the PRC and the Kandahar Air Wing, which maintains Mi-17s. This was going well, but there was a question about how effective that unit will be once its own mentors return home, as the demand on these assets will be very high.[15]

Joint Afghan Operations
In our interviews and fieldwork, we heard relatively few examples of joint operations between different Afghan SOF elements. One example, though, was a joint operation conducted by CF 333 and PRC Kapisa. The mentors at PRC Kapisa were aware of the advanced capa-

[13] Senior NCO, mentor force, March 10, 2013.

[14] PRC Kapisa mentor force, March 9, 2013.

[15] Junior officer, mentor force, March 3, 2013.

bilities of CF 333 and wanted to show PRC Kapisa "what right looks like." They consequently contacted their British counterparts and recommended that the two forces conduct a joint raid. The two units conducted mutually supportive and simultaneous raids on targets 300 meters apart. The execution of the two raids demonstrated vast differences in the respective unit's capabilities. For example, CF 333 conducted an independent assault on their target and was able to execute its own sensitive site exploitation, while PRC Kapisa struggled on both counts. The PRC, however, saw CF 333's capabilities as "something they can strive to be." It also helped build coordination that will be critical to the future of Afghan SOF capacity.[16]

Continuity and Pre-Mission Training

Continuity

As with the NMU mentors, the PRC mentors cited multiple rotations back to the same partner unit. Australian, Lithuanian, and, to a lesser extent, Romanian mentors have conducted multiple tours with the same partner unit. The Australians, for example, have worked with the PRC in Uruzgan for a number of years, with many mentors currently on their fourth tour. Accordingly, they have built strong personal relationships, not only with the PRC soldiers but also with Matiullah Khan, the Kandak Amniate Uruzgan's founder and current police chief of Uruzgan.[17] Lithuanians conducted four-month tours but generally deployed once per year or even more frequently. Despite the high turnover, they believed they have better continuity than units on single one-year tours because Lithuanian and Afghan soldiers all knew and recognized each other from trip to trip. They also see their approach as an improvement over the Kandahar PRC force, which has served as a kind of revolving door for mentors from a number of different nations, including units from Canada, the United States, and

---

[16] Interview with PRC Kapisa mentor force, March 9, 2013.

[17] Officer, mentor force, March 2, 2013. See also David Zucchino, "America's Go-to Man in Afghanistan's Oruzgan Province," *Los Angeles Times*, January 13, 2013.

now Lithuania. At the PRC in Kapisa, Romanian Special Forces were the continuity force, with a few members having worked at that location previously, including the partnering officer, who was described as beloved by the Afghan forces. The Romanians provided continuity because they were on a longer rotational cycle than the U.S. forces that worked with them.

A key issue regarding continuity is whether the incoming mentoring unit is able to pick up on the partnering mission where the previous unit left off, rather than repeat basics that have already been taught and learned. The Lithuanians, for example, reported that the PRC had sufficiently mastered individual tactical skills and that training would have to evolve to a focus on combined operations in a complex environment. They believed that their experience with multiple rotations helped achieve this perspective on continuity, so training does not start over and each new rotational unit but builds on previous efforts instead. At Kapisa, the U.S. team was rotating out while the two Romanian teams stayed in country to complete their longer tour cycles and so helped provide continuity across rotations.

Pre-Mission Training

PMT was an important part of preparation for PRC mentors, although, like NMU mentors, continuity in many cases made it less critical. Indeed, SOF teams were able to draw on prior experience in their partnering mission to enhance operational effectiveness. Repeat rotations definitely helped in this regard, as incoming teams already benefited from a prior work history with their Afghan partners. Teams were also able to draw on additional partnership experiences. The U.S. team leader at Kapisa was placed on the team in part because he previously mentored a different PRC in Afghanistan and had worked extensively with the Romanian SOF contingent in Europe. Other senior members of the team had experience in either Afghanistan or Iraq on a police training mission that mentors described as "the same but not the same" (meaning similar in basic requirements, such as rapport building, but different in specifics).[18]

---

[18] NCO, mentor force, March 10, 2013.

PMT for the PRC mentors varied. The U.S. team conducted a two-to-three-day training scenario on advising and training but otherwise focused on react-to-contact drills, because the team's parent unit focuses on close-quarters battle, and the team doesn't often get to practice the types of defensive engagements involved in a police SWAT mission. The Lithuanians also focused on individual and team skills but also incorporated a training exercise with a mock partner unit that consisted of a Lithuanian National Guard unit. Scenarios included the use of interpreters and simulated translation. The Lithuanians reported that this was excellent preparation for PRC operations. [19]

Summary

RAND visited only three of 19 PRCs in Afghanistan, so it is difficult to extrapolate all observations to the PRC force as a whole. However, one key theme that was evident in unit visits and seemed apparent in the overall PRC mentoring and command and control structure was that there was a high level of variability in both PRC capabilities and mentoring approaches. With 13 nations engaged in partnering with PRCs, there was inevitably going to be a high level of variation in mentorship approaches. Just considering task organization, the Australians in 2013 dedicated more than 200 men to mentoring a single PRC, the Lithuanians had a 60-man crew mentoring two PRCs, and then there was the Combined Special Operations Task Force 10 mission of combined U.S. and Eastern European SOF elements. These units also employ varying approaches to PMT, with the reliance on a mock partner force by the Lithuanians representing a notable best practice.

That said, there were several unifying observations. First, all the PRC mentors noted tensions over the need to achieve battlespace effects versus building PRC capacity. The balance in 2013 tilted toward an OPTEMPO focused on achieving operational effects, which may in turn inhibit unit development. All of the mentor units emphasized the importance of rapport, though the precise approach varies in the

---

[19] Junior officer, mentor force, March 3, 2013.

details. Certainly the repeat tours conducted by the Lithuanians, Australians, and, to a lesser extent, the Romanians aid in rapport as well as continuity. All of these units engage in non-transactional relationship building that emphasizes spending off time with Afghans. One challenge going forward, however, will be the impact of a reduction in coalition-provided logistical support on unit rapport. Several of the mentor units are also working on various ways to ease the Afghans toward transition by reducing the Afghan reliance on coalition-provided enablers.

CHAPTER FOUR

SOF Partnership in Afghanistan: The ANASOF Special Operations *Kandaks*

The Afghan MOD SOF capability is resident in ANASOC, a division-level formation in the ANA. ANASOC's primary operational units are nine battalion-sized formations referred to as special operations *kandaks* (SOKs). In addition to the SOKs, ANASOC has a Special Mission Wing (providing rotary lift), a military intelligence battalion, a support battalion, and a SOF School of Excellence.

Each SOK has three companies of ANA Commandos and one company of ANA Special Forces (ANASF). In addition, SOKs have a forward support company and, in theory, a military intelligence detachment (this latter capability was still being generated at the time of this writing). Commandos are an elite light-infantry force somewhat analogous to U.S. Army Rangers. The Commandos are designed to conduct specialized light-infantry operations, including reconnaissance, direct action, and internal defense operations. While the Commandos have conducted a range of missions in Afghanistan, they are commonly used to clear insurgents from key terrain areas held by the Afghan Local Police and in support of U.S. village stability operations (VSO).[1] ANASOC is in the process of establishing two brigade head-

---

[1] In VSO, U.S. special operations teams embed in rural areas of Afghanistan to establish local security, recruit and mentor Afghan Local Police, and promote local governance and development initiatives. The Afghan Local Police is a program of the Afghan MOI that seeks to recruit local defense forces from rural villages and districts in Afghanistan to provide security and defend against Taliban incursions.

quarters that will serve as a command and control function for the individual SOKs.

ANASF are explicitly modeled on U.S. Army Special Forces. They are intended to conduct a variety of mission sets, including air assault, reconnaissance, local civilian engagement via *shuras*, and information operations. The ANASF play a prominent role in helping U.S. forces recruit and mentor the Afghan Local Police.

Methodology

RAND analysts visited the 1st, 6th, and 8th SOKs. U.S. Army Special Forces teams mentored the 1st and 6th SOKs, and a U.S. Navy SEAL team mentored the 8th SOK. RAND analysts conducted interviews with U.S. military mentors and attached contractors, as well as Afghan officers and enlisted personnel. RAND analysts also interviewed CJSOTF-A personnel.

Partnering Approach

Task Organization

U.S. SOF teams from CJSOTF-A have had responsibility for partnering with the SOKs. Typically, the mentoring teams under this command include U.S. Army Special Forces ODAs, SEAL platoons, or Marine Special Operations Teams. During the research team's visit, the units varied in size, from 12 personnel on an ODA to more than 16 to 20 for a SEAL platoon. In addition, contractors and other enablers were attached to these units.

At the time, CJSOTF-A aligned a single special operations team, such as an ODA, a SEAL platoon, or a Marine Special Operations Team, with each Commando SOK (the command subsequently increased the number of teams allocated to each SOK). These teams typically assigned one or two unit members to mentor each Commando company through the training and operational cycles. This constant interface across training and operations reportedly paid "huge dividends," as the mentor's established rapport with the unit helped keep the Commandos motivated amid heavy fighting, and lessons learned from operations could then be easily integrated into to the training cycle.[2] The teams also assigned a senior operator to mentor the battalion commander. In one case, a chief warrant officer was chosen because of his senior status and his ability to focus full time on the battalion commander. In another case, the team commander played the role of battalion commander mentor, but these duties were also split with his role as operations planner and commander. CJSOTF-A also buttressed the training mission with contractors, referred to as the Logistics Training Team (LTT). The LTT assigned ten contracted mentors per SOK, who were charged with mentoring the battalion staff.[3]

The ODAs and the SEAL team RAND analysts met with worked hard to provide the Commando SOKs with necessary training and mentorship, but the alignment of a single SOF team to a SOK did present challenges. The first was force size. SEAL platoons have an advantage here, with 16 sailors (or more) to a team rather than the 12 soldiers assigned to an ODA. Special Forces doctrine calls for a single ODA to mentor a battalion-sized element, but as one interviewee noted, "[D]octrine fails to point out that this is a guerrilla battalion and not a professional force." He continued, "It takes more than 12 guys. Just mentorship alone with commanders, we don't have enough bodies to

---

[2]   1st SOK mentor, March 7, 2013.

[3]   Overall perceptions of the LTT seem to vary considerably. Some concerns have been expressed that the LTT overly relies on PowerPoint slides and lacks sufficient experience in mentoring battalion staffs. "We don't have time to teach LTT how to teach," observed one special operator. (Anonymous interview, date withheld.) Other teams, however, have come to rely on the LTT as a major force multiplier for a SOF team that is generally deemed as undermanned for the mission. As one lead SOF mentor noted, "LTTs are helping me every day. They give me a write up and inform me what is going on. . . . The LTT interact with partners on the staff, training the *kandak*, trying to enhance communication on the objectives. I can't do that; their importance is really significant." The SOF mentor went on to highlight the importance of fostering a strong working relationship with the LTT contractors: "I have looked across the other SOKs and don't see that mentality. I can't do it all." (Anonymous interview, date withheld.) His lead LTT mentor agrees: "[The SOF mentor] and I have a very good relationship that you don't see in other *kandaks*. Something we have always enjoyed with all the [SOF teams]." (Interview with LTT mentor, date withheld.)

do the mentoring."[4] This has been ameliorated by subsequent decisions in the summer of 2013 to assign two ODAs to every SOK (where SOKs are mentored by ODAs) but is an important lesson for future partnership efforts.

OPTEMPO is a major factor in this. At 1st SOK, the training and operational cycles were located at two different bases, with the majority of the partnered ODA situated with the green-cycle company (focused on operations). The 1st SOK's mentors had a high OPTEMPO akin to other *kandaks* and generally conducted an operation every week. As one Special Forces soldier observed, "Dudes up there [at the green-cycle compound] are smoked—if they are not training the Afghans they are planning two missions ahead."[5] It is not surprising that some suggested that this is a two-ODA mission, a conclusion accepted by SOJTF-A in the summer of 2013.

A second issue is rank structure. At the SOK, an ODA team captain (or chief warrant officer) must mentor a lieutenant colonel battalion commander. As an officer at CJSOTF-A noted, "The ODA team leaders are relatively young. The age gap makes it difficult for them to interact with Afghan battalion commanders."[6] To address this issue, CJSOTF-A has considered several alternatives, such as an ODA with an additional O-4 officer or attaching a full Special Forces company (referred to as an Advanced Operational Base, or AOB) to each of the SOKs. Shortage of AOBs and resistance to a nontraditional alignment of forces presents a challenge to executing either of these options.

Mission Focus

Given ongoing counterinsurgency operations, there has been a natural tension between attempting to achieve SOF effects on the battlefield through the *kandaks* and building *kandak* capacity. Interviews with the special operations teams as well as with CJSOTF-A suggest, however, that OPTEMPO has overridden a focus on *kandak* capacity building. It has already been mentioned that a high OPTEMPO

---

[4]   Anonymous interview, date withheld.

[5]   1st SOK mentor, March 6, 2013.

[6]   CJSOTF-A officer, March 8, 2013.

at 1st SOK consumed much of the time and attention of the ODA, as they typically planned three missions out and conducted an operation a week. Other teams agreed with this assessment. One special operator observed, "Our mission is to train . . . [the] SOK to unilateral capability while maintaining our operational cycle. We support VSO with operations. There is no balance between the two. . . . We can't train when we do operations."[7] He continued, "You are trying to train and run operations with one SOF team and it is a lot to do. First thing to go is training." Such a challenge was readily identified at CJSOTF-A, where early guidance in the campaign was to "grab an Afghan face to do operations with" without concern about building Afghan capability.[8] Even currently, however, several teams felt that they were primarily judged on the operational effects they achieved rather than the capability they were able to impart on the *kandaks*.

This OPTEMPO focus has had several negative effects on *kandak* capability. First, as the quotes above suggest, teams have had little time to focus on training. Furthermore, as a senior CJSOTF-A officer suggested, "Transferring knowledge is hard when being shot at."[9] Second, complex operations seemed to overtax the ability of Afghans to retain knowledge. This was especially so since most Afghan units will never be able to sustain the multiday and helicopter-borne operations that were recently in common practice. Most importantly, many operations were driven by the special operations teams and the special operations task forces and so were nearly completely dependent on U.S. intelligence and operational planning.[10] The result was that *kandaks* did not gain experience in mission planning, and their drive to develop their own intelligence was undercut. As one special operator noted,

> If we are going to do this, somebody needs to make a decision [on whether we should focus on operations or training]. . . . The

---

[7] Anonymous interview, date withheld.

[8] CJSOTF-A officer, March 8, 2013.

[9] CJSOTF-A officer, March 8, 2013.

[10] Special operations task forces are subordinate to CJSOTF-A and are aligned to different regions of Afghanistan.

[*kandaks*] can't develop their own intel, so we are pushing them to do our operations. We are giving them our intel; that makes sure we are out there on the ground and do what we have been doing, pushing them to complete the mission and sometimes taking the lead when they stumble and fall. So somebody make a decision.[11]

Indeed, at the time of our fieldwork, CJSOTF-A was on the verge of making just such a decision. However, subsequent decisions have limited the change in OPTEMPO. This is in large part due to the perceived need for continued SOF effects, especially during the retrograde of U.S. and coalition forces. Post-2014 evaluations will be needed to determine how much this may have negatively affected partner-force development.

Rapport

All the U.S. teams visited readily recognized the importance of rapport with their Afghan counterparts and spoke of the different ways they seek to build rapport. At 8th SOK, an LTT mentor observed, "Rapport is a critical enabler. Nothing can be accomplished without it. [You] need to show interest in the personal relationship, although that is difficult due to cultural differences."[12] To this end, some SEAL mentors made a point to take one day a week spending off-duty time with the Afghans and not talking about work: "Devote some time specifically to personal interaction only—no business."[13]

The 6th SOK mentors would likely agree with this approach. One team member observed how the Afghans "hate how we go down there only for business. Sometime we put [traditional Afghan garments] on and go down for tea and they love that [stuff]."[14] The ODA also described efforts at sharing stories with the Afghans, asking about their

---

[11] Anonymous interview, date withheld.

[12] LTT mentor, March 3, 2013.

[13] LTT mentor, March 3, 2013.

[14] NCO mentor, March 4, 2013.

families and even wrestling. They added to this the need to lead by example and show that they are effective on missions.[15]

Similar approaches characterize the rapport-building activities at 1st SOK. Furthermore, one factor aiding relationships at the 1st SOK amber (training) camp is the relative close proximity between the ODA compound and the Afghan camp. The short distance facilitated interactions between the ODA mentors and the Commandos. The visiting RAND analysts especially saw the benefits, as Afghan commanders could easily visit the facility for study interviews, and the RAND team enjoyed the ability to interact with Afghan soldiers and observe training events. At the urging of an Afghan officer, analysts also enjoyed lunch in the Afghan mess hall.

Key Tasks

The purpose of this section is to provide a short review of some of the key partnering tasks undertaken with the various SOF teams interviewed for this report.

Logistics

Due to the frequent problems endemic to the Afghan logistics system, many of the SOKs suffered shortages in fuel, spare parts, ammunition, and other needed supplies. Across the *kandaks* we interviewed, there was consensus that, at this stage in the Afghan campaign, partner units can no longer afford to circumvent supply shortages with coalition-provisioned materials. This was a lesson learned at the 1st and 6th SOKs, where prior teams had made a habit of providing supplies. One 6th SOK mentor said there was a natural, and likely learned, tendency among the Afghans to ask for supplies. He noted breaking this habit was like "breaking the baby from the pacifier." As a consequence, "We refuse to give them anything. Our job is not to provide them with material things."[16]

This does not mean, however, that teams cannot mentor Afghans in improving their logistics systems. Indeed, the LTT mentors were

---

[15] NCO mentor, March 4, 2013.

[16] 6th SOK mentors, March 3, 2013.

crucial in this regard and learned to draw on their broad mentorship network to work supply issues across multiple echelons. At the 1st SOK, for example, the lead LTT mentor was preparing to conduct an engagement with the logistics (or S-4) staff and mentors at ANASOC to understand the reasoning for fuel shortages and to identify new mentorship opportunities to address the problem.[17]

Intelligence

The lack of organic intelligence inputs was a major problem in the SOKs, a problem potentially spurred by U.S.-driven operations that relied heavily on U.S.-provided intelligence. To address this shortfall, ANASOC created a military intelligence battalion to enhance organic intelligence capabilities, but these units will likely not be fully fielded until late 2014.[18] In the meantime, the mentors at 8th SOK worked hard to connect the 8th SOK to existent Afghan intelligence sources, such as the NDS and even conventional ANA.[19]

Operational Planning

Most Commando missions have been tasked by U.S. SOF and driven by U.S. intelligence and approved with U.S.-crafted concepts of operations. As a result, Afghan commanders have limited opportunity to practice mission planning. The mission brief to Afghan commanders has thus been a rare opportunity to mentor planning skills. RAND analysts were able to observe one mission brief where a U.S. officer pro-

---

[17] 1st SOK LTT mentor, March 6, 2013.

[18] U.S. Department of Defense, *Progress Toward Security and Stability in Afghanistan*, Washington, D.C., April 2014, p. 42.

[19] 8th SOK mentors, February 27, 2013. There are varied intelligence capabilities within the Afghan government. Conventional ANA units have organic intelligence assets. At the interagency level, there is the NDS and the NTEC. There are also the Operations Coordination Centers at the provincial level (OCC-Ps), which are intended to be the hub for Afghan interagency coordination, with representation from ANA, Afghan National Police, and the NDS. The SOKs, however, were not well connected to these entities. Breaking down the walls between Afghan government agencies was a top priority at CJSOTF-A. It has also been recommended that the ANASF play a more-prominent role in intelligence collection, though the human intelligence capacity of such forces reportedly needs to be upgraded.

vided detailed and directed guidance to the Afghan officer on how the Afghans were to conduct the operation.

In other cases, however, the mission brief was used as a teachable moment. As one SOF team noted, "We are trying to give them ownership, less dictatorship. . . . We discuss plans with the company commander, he gives us his idea of plan, and we make suggestions as necessary. If he wants everyone facing and shooting each other, we will present other options. We don't say you are wrong, just what do you think about [this other option]?"[20] The Afghan commander agreed that this was the approach taken, noting that the SOF team provided an enemy situation and then they "make the plan together." He continued, "They use the Commando plan. If first time they see my plan it is not a good plan they are asking what do you think if you do it like this? I think 'okay, good.' We are talking about finding the best way [that] is for our benefit."[21]

Continuity and Pre-Mission Training

Continuity

Continuity of operations is a unique challenge for U.S. SOF partnership operations in Afghanistan. Unlike many of the international units that partner with GDPSU units, U.S. special operations commanders have not instituted a policy of routinely returning the same SOF teams to partner units. Many of the special operators we interviewed have been on multiple deployments to Afghanistan, but relatively few of these deployments have returned operators to the same partner units. As a result, new units must work to forge relationships with each rotation, a time-consuming process. As a senior CJSOTF-A officer noted, the U.S. unit's lack of long-term relationships was not productive: "We walk away."[22] Many of the partner teams adamantly agree. "We thrive

---

[20] Anonymous interview, date withheld.

[21] Anonymous interview with Afghan officer, date withheld.

[22] CJSOTF-A officer, March 8, 2013.

off [of] partnership," observed one Special Forces soldier. "There is no effort to get guys back to the same location."[23]

CJSOTF-A was quick to identify this as an issue and expressed frustration that it does not control the request for forces fill, which is ultimately sourced by U.S. Special Operations Command and the service providers. Various reasons have been attributed as to why units do not return to the same location. For example, it has been argued that there is an effort to more evenly allocate the mentoring-combat experience across the force. Whatever the reason, a CJSOTF-A officer wistfully hoped that this would eventually change, noting that CJSOTF-A was attempting to align ODAs to specific partner commands: "Maybe in the 2015 environment there will be more long-term unit connections. Maybe."[24]

Another related concern expressed with regard to continuity was the fact that partnering operations "start over" with each new incoming SOF team. Because new units lack familiarity with their partners, they usually reset training to the basics because they are not "comfortable" with the unit's capabilities. Even an LTT contractor observed this when he noted that the "problem with military rotation, [is] every time they rotate out you just start over again; it is like Groundhog Day."[25] Part of this problem stems from not returning units to Afghan partners. It also has to do with an ad hoc assessment approach utilized by the *kandak* partners. This assessment process was typically described as evaluating lessons learned during partnered Commando operations and then retooling training to address observed shortfalls. Such an approach does not convey unit progress across rotations or across *kandaks*. As a CJSOTF-A officer noted, there needs to be a higher-level assessment that can carry over rotations, get passed on during handover, and thus enable "the new team [to push] to the next milestone instead of repeating the same do loop."[26]

---

[23] Anonymous interview, date withheld.

[24] CJSOTF-A officer, March 8, 2013.

[25] LTT mentor, date withheld.

[26] CJSOTF-A officer, March 8, 2013.

To help compensate for these shortfalls, teams must work hard to effectively transfer information across incoming and outgoing teams. The ODA mentoring 1st SOK, for example, relied on frequent phone calls with the deployed team and reviewed storyboards, operation summaries, after-action reports, and lessons learned from every operation. The chief warrant officer mentor was in touch with the officer who would replace him. Even so, the current ODA gained some valuable lessons learned from the RIP. When arriving, the ODA team was aware that there were problems with the *kandak* but were surprised at the extent of them. They also did not have insight on what the predecessor unit did to resolve the problems.

The LTT contractors present another key resource. Many of these contractors remained on the job for years at a time and so offered an expansive view of how the unit developed over time. As one contractor observed, "At my smaller level with ODAs, a lot of these guys don't have a good left-right handoff. We try to bridge that gap."[27] It is unclear how much, if any, LTT presence will remain post-2014, making this a potential shortfall.

Pre-Mission Training
PMT varied across the interviewed units. The 8th SOK mentors, for example, noted that they received no training specific to their partnering mission and commented that such training would have been especially valuable given that FID is not a typical SEAL mission.[28] Alternatively, 1st SOK mentors commented that their PMT included a practice FID exercise with an Army reconnaissance squadron serving as the FID force. The lead mentor noted that it was the "best training I ever had."[29]

---

[27] LTT mentor, March 4, 2013.

[28] 8th SOK mentors, February 27, 2013.

[29] 1st SOK mentor, March 7, 2013.

Summary

Overall, the Commando SOKs have developed tactical proficiency within their units, though several key challenges remain. First, integration of Afghan intelligence into operational planning remains a significant shortfall and has been abetted in part by reliance on U.S.-derived intelligence and operational planning. Second, the Commando SOKs have continued to maintain a high OPTEMPO that has limited the focus on training SOK capability. The main challenge here is that a high OPTEMPO directs the time and attention of U.S. mentors toward planning and execution of operations, rather than unit training. This problem was made more acute by the assignment of a single SOF team, enabled with contractors, to mentor an entire battalion.

CHAPTER FIVE
SOF Partnership in Iraq

This chapter presents an analysis of U.S. SOF efforts to partner with and build the capability of Iraqi SOF from 2003 to 2012. It begins with a brief overview of U.S. SOF work with Iraqi SOF during Operation Iraqi Freedom and Operation New Dawn, based on open-source materials. This overview is not intended to be a comprehensive history of U.S. SOF in Iraq. Its purpose is to provide context for the subsequent section, which summarizes not-for-attribution interviews conducted by RAND analysts with a sample of members from the U.S. Army Special Forces and Navy SEAL teams who conducted partnering operations with Iraqi SOF.

Methodology

This chapter uses both primary and secondary source material. RAND personnel conducted interviews with 26 U.S. SOF personnel who had partnered with Iraqi SOF. These interviews took place from February through April 2013. The period of Iraq deployments in this sample ranged from 2004 to 2012. Almost all of the interviewees had multiple deployments to Iraq (many to both Iraq and Afghanistan) and ranged in rank from E-6 to O-4. Iraqi partner units included the Iraqi Counterterrorism Task Force (ICTF), the 36th Commando Battalion, ISOF, various Iraqi Special Weapons and Tactics units, various regional commando battalions, and the Counter-Terrorism Command (CTC). In addition, this chapter draws on journalistic accounts and unclassified U.S. government publications detailing SOF partnership in Iraq.

Overview and Task Organization of SOF Partnership

The use of U.S. SOF to build Iraqi partner capability began after the initial invasion of Operation Iraqi Freedom. At that time, a Coalition Provisional Authority (CPA) directive disbanded the Iraqi Army and all other military forces.[1] This meant that new Iraqi security forces needed to be built from the ground up. U.S. Army Special Forces trainers placed their initial focus on the Iraqi Civil Defense Corps, which later became the Iraqi National Guard and then the Iraqi Army. In September 2003, the CPA established the ICTF.[2] It would eventually become the Iraqi Special Operations Force (ISOF).

Until the government of Iraq took operational control of ISOF in September 2006 (as well control of all other Iraqi Security Forces), U.S. SOF were fully in charge of ISOF training and equipping and played a significant role in recruitment and selection. In addition to direct partnering in Iraq, training of the ICTF was initially conducted in Jordan, which reportedly reduced security risks and helped promote operational capabilities. The Jordanian training venues were used until proper Iraqi facilities could be constructed, resulting in the Iraqi Special Warfare Center and School.[3]

Early reports suggested that ISOF was maturing into a proficient force quickly. As early as July 2005, the U.S. Department of Defense reported that "ISOF elements have been conducting operations for the past year. They have played crucial roles in major combat operations along side of, and sometimes independently of, Coalition forces."[4] Visiting Baghdad in 2006, former Assistant Secretary of Defense Bing

---

[1]   L. Paul Bremer, "Coalition Provisional Authority Order Number 2," *IraqCoalition.org*, May 23, 2003.

[2]   Andrew Rathmell, Olga Oliker, Terrence K. Kelly, David Brannan, and Keith Crane, *Developing Iraq's Security Sector: The Coalition Provisional Authority's Experience*, Santa Monica, Calif.: RAND Corporation, MG-365-OSD, 2005, p. 34.

[3]   Michael O'Brien, "Foreign Internal Defense in Iraq: ASOF Core Tasks Enable Iraqi Combating-Terrorism Capability," *Special Warfare*, January–March 2012, p. 25. Within Iraqi organization charts, it falls under the "Academia" unit or brigade.

[4]   U.S. Department of Defense, "Report to Congress: Measuring Stability and Security in Iraq," Washington, D.C., July 2005, p. 13.

West described the SOF operations that included Iraqis as one of the few "bright spots" to be found during that stage of the conflict.[5] In 2007, the Independent Commission on the Security Forces of Iraq reported that "Iraqi Special Operations are the most capable element of the Iraqi armed forces and are well-trained in both individual and collective skills. They are currently capable of leading counterterrorism operations, but they continue to require Coalition support."[6]

However, coalition concerns were beginning to emerge in April 2007 after the Iraqi prime minister signed Directive 61, declaring ISOF independent of both the MOD and MOI.[7] ISOF was placed under the CTC, which in turn reported to the Counter-Terrorism Service (CTS).[8] The CTS reported to the Office of the Commander in Chief (OCINC)—an extra-constitutional body that has not been approved by the Council of Representatives and reports directly to the prime minister—instead of the MOD.[9] The OCINC was widely perceived to be a "shadow headquarters" that was dedicated to pursuing a sectarian agenda.[10] Additionally, the government of Iraq began an effort to triple the authorized size of the ISOF and CTS, from about 1,600 personnel

---

[5] Bing West, *The Strongest Tribe: War, Politics, and the Endgame in Iraq*, New York: Random House, 2008, p. 190.

[6] James Jones, *The Report of the Independent Commission on the Security Forces of Iraq*, Washington, D.C, September 6, 2007, p. 63.

[7] "9010 Report," dated January 9, 2009, p. 52.

[8] The CTS was originally called the Counter-Terrorism *Bureau* (CTB) when first mentioned in the June 7, 2007, iteration of the U.S. Department of Defense's "Measuring Stability and Security in Iraq" report to Congress. The November 4, 2009, report began referring to it as the CTS.

[9] Office of the Special Inspector General for Iraq Reconstruction, *Iraqi Security Forces: Special Operations Program Is Achieving Goals, but Iraqi Support Remains Critical to Success*, Arlington, Va., SIGIR 11-004, October 25, 2010, p. 15. Also see International Crisis Group, "Loose Ends: Iraq's Security Forces Between U.S. Drawdown and Withdrawal," Middle East Report no. 99, October 26, 2010, pp. 12–17.

[10] Michael Gordon and Bernard Trainor, *The Endgame: The Inside Story of the Struggle for Iraq, from George W. Bush to Barack Obama*, New York: Random House, 2012, pp. 360–361; Office of the Special Inspector General for Iraq Reconstruction, 2010, p. 15.

in May 2006 to approximately 4,800 by January 2008.[11] Although a memorandum of agreement provided for the MOD to pay salaries and provide equipment to the units within the CTC, problems with pay and supplies quickly emerged under the new structure.[12]

In May 2008, CTS's authorized strength was again doubled to more than 8,500 personnel, adding force structure that included four regional commando battalions that were each authorized 440 soldiers.[13] The ISOF subsequently went from units with some of the highest assigned strengths and best retention rates to experiencing problems with both recruiting and retention. In March 2009, the ISOF was manned at 67 percent. To bring the ISOF to full strength, in June 2009 the minister of defense was ordered to transfer 1,400 soldiers from the Army to CTS, but as of January 2010 no transfers had occurred. Management problems within the CTS may have exacerbated the assigned strength problems. Due to budget shortfalls, in April 2009 the ISOF specialty pay of $800 per month was suspended.[14]

The penultimate edition of the series of U.S. Department of Defense reports to Congress, "Measuring Stability and Security in Iraq" (often called the "9010 Reports"), stated that CTS had a projected end strength of 9,200 personnel but its manning level was only 59 percent "due to budget shortfalls, a hiring freeze, and a need for specialized training." Nonetheless, the assessment stated that CTS remained "a highly capable force that contributes significantly to the [counterinsurgency] effort."[15]

---

[11] "9010 Reports," dated May 26, 2006, p. 55; September 14, 2007, p. 44; and March 7, 2008, p. 31.

[12] "9010 Report," dated September 26, 2008, p. 57; interview with U.S. Special Forces soldier, date withheld.

[13] Office of the Special Inspector General for Iraq Reconstruction, 2010, p. 16.

[14] Office of the Special Inspector General for Iraq Reconstruction, 2010, p. 17; and "9010 Report," dated November 4, 2009, p. 64.

[15] "9010 Report," dated January 29, 2010, pp. 43, 68. (This series of reports remained commonly known as the "9010 Report" even after the relevant section number in subsequent defense appropriations acts changed.)

Combat missions in Iraq by U.S. conventional forces were halted on August 31, 2010. U.S. SOF, however, continued performing counterterrorism missions paired with ISOF throughout 2011—until such operations were transitioned fully to ISOF on December 15, 2011, when the headquarters of U.S. Forces–Iraq was transitioned out.[16] Subsequent U.S. SOF activities in Iraq would be part of a "standard military to military relationship" under the Office of Security Cooperation–Iraq, located in U.S. Embassy–Baghdad.[17] In at least one case, the Iraqi government requested that a U.S. SOF unit advise Iraqi SOF on counterterrorism and intelligence.[18]

Partnering Approach

Task Organization

The task organization for SOF partnership in Iraq was generally similar to the SOK partnership in Afghanistan. Typically, an ODA or SEAL platoon from the CJSOTF Arabian Peninsula (CJSOTF-AP) would be partnered with an Iraqi SOF unit. Rotation lengths varied to some extent but were typically about six months.

Mission Focus

In line with the anticipated mission of ISOF, U.S. partnering focused on direct action and special reconnaissance missions. Interviews, however, attest to the varying degrees to which U.S. efforts allowed the Iraqis to more actively develop unilateral capability.

---

[16] Dave Butler, "Lights Out: ARSOF Reflect on Eight Years in Iraq," *Special Warfare*, January–March 2012, p. 30. The United States stopped mentoring the Emergency Response Brigade, which fell under the MOI, in mid-2011.

[17] Butler, 2012, p. 32.

[18] Tim Arango, "Syrian War's Spillover Threatens a Fragile Iraq," *New York Times*, September 24, 2012, p. A1. According to the 2013 Budget Summary issued by the White House, functions of the Office of Security Cooperation–Iraq included serving as the cornerstone for "cooperation on counterterrorism" as well as other security cooperation activities. See U.S. Office of Management and Budget, "Overseas Contingency Operations," in *Fiscal Year 2013 Budget of the U.S. Government*, 2012, p. 91.

According to one set of interviews, early development of the ICTF began with a one-to-one ratio of U.S. to Iraqi SOF during operations; U.S. mentors would walk ICTF teams through rehearsals, but back off to some distance during operations, maintaining radio communications to provide the ICTF teams with reachback. Eventually, the mentors would just "hand off the mission and let the ICTF teams loose to conduct the operation."[19] A former mentor stated that there must be a conscious effort to guide the partner force through all the developmental steps: "It's like watching a kid grow up and have the chance to fail and learn from his mistakes."[20]

In contrast, others reported that U.S. mentors would not let Iraqi SOF take the lead because the priority was to "get to the target," not develop ICTF capability.[21] Some mentors stated that there was a tendency to continually jump in instead of allowing ICTF processes to operate from planning to completion. Phrases like *by, with, for; doing it ourselves, partnering, enabling*; or *partnering, enabling, independent* were often used but not understood by everyone as having the same meanings. One interviewee suggested that developing Iraqi SOF took a lower priority than conducting strikes because the U.S. military thought that Iraq would be stable before U.S. forces left. Others suggested that some U.S. units were reluctant to let the Iraqis conduct unilateral operations in part because of a natural desire to take an active role in the fight rather than remain on base during missions.[22] From this perspective, the desire to be involved in the mission biased estimates of manning requirements.

Beyond tactical support, interviews suggested that U.S. mentorship to senior leaders and staff, as well as SOF support units, was limited. First, the United States was reportedly late in mentoring Iraqi SOF senior leaders and staff. Interviewees stated that the Iraqi tactical

---

[19] NCO, Ft. Meade, April 9, 2013.

[20] NCO, Ft. Meade, April 9, 2013.

[21] NCO, Ft. Meade, April 9, 2013.

[22] NCO, Ft. Meade, April 9, 2013.

operators were very good and the first priority for training.[23] However, interviewees also noted that "direct action is what SOF likes to do" and felt that U.S. SOF tend to be biased toward developing this aspect of partner capability.[24] Solid staff work is a vital necessity for partners to be able to sustain their operational abilities. As one former mentor described it, rather than building staffing capability, U.S. SOF "was too focused on blowing in doors and getting the bad guys instead of command and staff development."[25] As the lead was being transferred to Iraqis, the gaps in staff planning ability were apparent. The Iraqis did not understand basic planning processes and, more critically, did not understand how to tie in logistics, personnel, and intelligence to operations.

A related problem concerned training and capability of ISOF support units. ISOF support units did not achieve the same level of capability as the ISOF action units. There was a problem with recruitment and training for these units. These were critical skills, but few Iraqi personnel wanted to be "the guy wearing NODs [night observation device] driving a truck with 20 assaulters in the back."[26] After a bad experience when several Iraqi troops were killed in a vehicle accident, the mentors created a formal driver training course. Completing driver qualification became a point of pride, and all the Iraqi SOF personnel wanted to take the course.

Rapport

Developing rapport with the partner force was universally stated to be a critical requirement. Rapport was frequently mentioned as an important element of force protection, but was also deemed important to achieve the goals of capability development and conducting partnered operations.

---

[23] NCO, Ft. Meade, April 9, 2013.

[24] NCO, Ft. Meade, April 9, 2013.

[25] NCO, Ft. Meade, April 9, 2013.

[26] NCO, Ft. Meade, April 9, 2013.

A number of operators commented on the importance of Arabic-language skills. First, it was suggested that even basic survival-level knowledge of Arabic was useful in building rapport. Some interviewees went so far as to argue that it would be ideal to have advanced Arabic skills, so as to negate the need for outside interpreters. Others argued that no matter how proficient an American soldier can be with a language—even if he is a 3/3 on the U.S. Defense Language Proficiency Test—it was necessary to have an interpreter to capture the subtleties, nuances, and tone necessary to effective communication.[27]

None of the interviewees reported knowledge of even a single "insider attack" (where a local security force soldier would attack an American mentor) in ISOF units. As such, there was no "guardian angel" requirement.[28] Still, interviewees said that at least one armed person would keep an eye on partner force personnel but were not set aside for this task in an obvious manner. However, all members of the team would usually have their weapons loaded with a round in the chamber. A common technique among mentors during high-level meetings was to carry a pistol concealed under the uniform blouse in an unobtrusive manner. Except during missions, U.S. SOF interviewed reported they typically did not wear body armor when working with their Iraqi partner force. Developing trust and rapport with the partner force was commonly reported as being the best force-protection measure.

Key Tasks

This section provides a short review of some of the key approaches undertaken with the various SOF teams interviewed.

---

[27] The first number is listening, and the second is speaking. A "3" is usually the highest rating on the U.S. Defense Language Proficiency Test. However, in some languages the highest is a "4," which indicates ability to listen or speak at a postgraduate level.

[28] This is a technique required in Afghanistan by ISAF in Afghanistan. It requires that at least one person in every group interacting with Afghans outside a coalition base be designated to carry a weapon in "red" status (loaded with a round in the chamber, safety off) and provide overwatch while having no other duties, such as participating in conversations or giving instructions, and usually wearing body armor.

Logistics

Logistics was commonly mentioned as a significant shortfall that did not get adequately resolved during eight years of partnering. It "was their [the Iraqis'] Achilles' heel."[29] There were problems in all classes of supply due to a combination of a failure to anticipate operational requirements and to request supplies as well as distribution problems. Iraqi leaders tended to hoard supplies at different levels, claiming that they did so because of the unreliability of the supply flow. Additionally, they often blamed this practice on uncertainty regarding how long coalition forces would be there to help them obtain items. The "Iraqis were dependent upon [U.S. forces]" at the start, then "it became hard to wean them off our support."[30]

U.S. SOF initially built an Iraqi SOF combat force but did not build a combat service support structure to go with it. It was not until 2009 that Iraqi logistics and support needs began to receive an emphasis for capability development. A common refrain was that "the greatest obstacle to completing the mission was logistics."[31] This became an even greater problem after ISOF were realigned under the prime minister instead of the MOD. Some U.S. SOF perceived that this caused the Iraqi SOF to have a lower priority for support from the MOD, and thus funding and other support intended for SOF were channeled to conventional forces. Further, this heightened distrust of SOF by the conventional forces and their command structures. One interviewee suggested that even a typical "third world country looks at its own SOF as a threat."[32] There was no consensus on whether the cause was corruption, distrust, lack of competence, or a combination thereof, but the apparent disconnect between the MOD and Iraqi SOF was frequently mentioned by U.S. SOF working at Iraqi brigade and higher levels during later rotations.

---

[29] 5th SFG personnel, Ft. Campbell, March 5, 2013.

[30] 5th SFG personnel, Ft. Campbell, March 5, 2013.

[31] 5th SFG personnel, Ft. Campbell, March 5, 2013.

[32] 5th SFG personnel, Ft. Campbell, March 5, 2013.

Former mentors also asserted that the ISOF had gotten too used to the United States stepping in to fix problems for them. Thus, the stage was not set for attaining self-sufficiency. Issuing only U.S. equipment to ISOF made training and conducting combined strike operations easier and provided a higher level of capability during partnering. However, it exacerbated the problem of developing an independent capability, as the Iraqi logistics system and general expertise were both more aligned to ex–Warsaw Pact equipment (e.g., AK-47s are easier to support than M-4s). Also, an interviewee returning from a recent deployment stated that since U.S. Foreign Military Sales were conducted on behalf of the MOI and MOD, the move to put CTS under the prime minister further highlighted the longer-term challenge of using U.S. equipment.

Intelligence

A particular area of staffing problems concerned intelligence, specifically J-2 (intelligence) and J-6 (communications) capability and coordination. ISOF had some signals intelligence (SIGINT) capabilities development in terms of "push to talk" collection capability with (nonclassified) commercially available systems. However, these were not sustainable—particularly due to lack of technical maintenance capability. No field service representatives or contracted maintenance support was put into place: "So, the Iraqis would use the stuff until it broke and cannibalize the parts they could. By the end of a rotation, 50 percent of the equipment was non–mission capable."[33]

Intelligence staff development also lagged. Intelligence and targeting packages provided by U.S. forces allowed a "spin and grin" approach, wherein everything was handed over to the ISOF, with no analysis required.[34] This did not create an understanding of how to turn information into intelligence and what to do with intelligence once developed. Interviewees stated that the Iraqis "were somewhat better with HUMINT [human intelligence]" but were lacking in a

---

[33] Former NCO, Ft. Meade, April 9, 2013.

[34] Asymmetric Warfare Group personnel, Ft. Meade, April 9, 2013.

number of other areas of intelligence.[35] Nonetheless, former mentors stated that "Iraqi SOF are very good at making sense of atmospherics" (e.g., detecting abnormal patterns of life in a home or neighborhood).[36] Some interviewees reported that the Iraqis were better at this aspect of understanding the operational environment than U.S. SOF.

Leadership Development

Iraqi senior leaders, including general officers, often lacked knowledge of and experience with senior management skills even when they otherwise displayed good leadership ability. Interviewees stated that the U.S. SOF units frequently assigned mentors who were too junior in rank to their counterparts to be effective. They stated that in theory, coalition general officers also have a mentoring role with partner general officers. In practice, however, they usually did not spend enough time with them and did not develop the personal relationships necessary to be an effective mentor.

Another challenge was that in many cases, interviewees reported that Iraqi junior officers were not leading their troops. It was a cultural problem to begin with and became worse as nepotism increased. It was suggested that a typical lieutenant would just show up for the operation and want a seat on the truck but would not eat, live, or train with his men. This did not happen as often or was easier to fix during earlier periods, when U.S. SOF selected the leadership. One technique used was to have a U.S. SOF O-3 mentor the Iraqi lieutenant and encourage him to lead by example. In a few cases, it was reported that having a U.S. mentor at the O-3 level speak to the lieutenant's Iraqi battalion or brigade commander had a salutary effect.

Nepotism and politicization were frequently mentioned problems after the Iraqi government took full control over its various SOF elements. Interviewees reported that the ICTF was a highly capable and elite force when coalition forces played the leading role in the selection process and targeting. After the prime minister took control, however, the ISOF increasingly became perceived as a sectarian tool. It

---

[35] Former NCO, Ft. Meade, April 9, 2013.

[36] Senior NCO, Ft. Meade, April 9, 2013.

appeared that more officers were assigned for nepotistic reasons and so were unqualified for their positions. One interviewee reported that the CTC commander at the time was a political appointee with no SOF experience or background. Another claimed that "nepotism is damaging unit pride" because unqualified leaders were being appointed.[37] Mentors pushed for transparency in the process and made recommendations regarding qualified officers for vacant positions, but reported they had declining leverage and influence in later rotations.

Sectarianism

Mentors with the most-recent deployments frequently reported sectarianism to be an increasing challenge. Specifically, U.S. SOF personnel stated they believed that an implicit rule, implemented after coalition forces lost oversight of the ISOF following security transition, was that all targets must be Sunni and that the prime minister would not allow the CTS to target Shi'a threats. While this assertion is rejected by the CTS, other Iraqis believe it to be true, highlighting that, at a minimum, CTS operations lack a clear legal framework.[38]

Continuity and Pre-Mission Training

Continuity

Continuity in partnering arrangements was widely held to be a valuable approach when possible. For example, several interviewees stated that their company had worked with the same partner unit for more than seven years. They "were able to watch Iraqi captains get promoted all the way up to general."[39] In cases where many of the same U.S. SOF individuals did not have repeated rotations with the same Iraqi coun-

---

[37] Senior NCO, Ft. Meade, April 9, 2013.

[38] See Richard Brennan Jr., Charles P. Ries, Larry Hanauer, Ben Connable, Terrence K. Kelly, Michael J. McNerney, Stephanie Young, Jason Campbell, and K. Scott McMahon, *Ending the U.S. War in Iraq: The Final Transition, Operational Maneuver, and Disestablishment of United States Forces–Iraq*, Santa Monica Calif.: RAND Corporation, RR-232-USFI, 2013, pp. 186–189.

[39] 5th SFG personnel, Ft. Campbell, March 5, 2013.

terparts, it was still valuable to have a routine relationship between U.S. SOF headquarters and ISOF headquarters. This helped to establish a common baseline understanding of Iraqi partner capabilities and the training they needed. Otherwise, new rotations had a tendency to start from scratch and build their own assessment of their Iraqi partners and retrain skills that had already been mastered. When there was continuity in individual mentors or U.S. SOF headquarters, interviewees reported that the Iraqi units progressed more rapidly because their training programs would keep moving forward instead of pausing or regressing as each new mentor rotation took a step back to assess.

A good handover between mentor rotations was widely reported as a critical task. This was simplified when the rotations were between units with a mutual higher headquarters. In such cases, the individuals in both rotations knew each other personally. Plus, they were likely to be on a future rotation back to the same partner unit and wanted to pay forward a good handover back to themselves in the future.

A technique that several interviewees mentioned as being effective was to make "baseball cards" for all of the Iraqi SOF personnel in the partner unit and then pass these to the new rotation. This usually entailed making a 3" x 5" card with a short biography and observations about each Iraqi SOF unit member, but variations included formats of other sizes or Excel spreadsheets. The idea was to help incoming mentors quickly learn about their Iraqi partners and pass on key information such as perceived trustworthiness and personal connections.

Especially problematic rotations were mentioned as the result of poor handover between companies or battalions from different Special Forces groups and SEAL platoons from different teams. In two cases described during interviews, the group/team of the incoming mentors was focused on direct action and the conduct of strike operations, whereas the outgoing group/team had placed an emphasis on FID and building independent capability within their Iraqi partner units. This led to significant disruption of the partner-force relationship.

Pre-Mission Training

Respondents expressed some mixed points of view in terms of the value of FID-focused PMT. Most Special Forces interviewees reported that their PMT was routine because FID is a core Special Forces mission—they did not feel the need for a particular focus on this skill. In a few cases however, Special Forces operators lamented that a direct action–oriented PMT was less useful for their rotations. In contrast, interviewed SEAL operators suggested that FID is not a typical mission and that PMT that prepared them for FID would have been useful. As one SEAL noted, "[The FID mission] requires a change in mindset."[40] In one instance, a SEAL platoon leader reported that his PMT was purely about direct action, and, when it came time to train their Iraqi partners, they were at a disadvantage.

Interviews suggested three helpful components of FID-focused PMT. First, operators found the use of a mock partner forces in PMT particularly useful. These mock partner units were typically drawn from conventional units and helped to build training skills. In at least one instance, soldiers from the 101st Airborne were used as the mock partner force, though it was advised that it would have been best to have a mock force that hailed from a non-infantry unit that was less tactically proficient. Second, SOF operators noted that PMT was most valuable when the deploying unit knew the specifics of its upcoming partners. In cases where there was continuity in partnerships or when the mentor unit otherwise knew exactly what Iraqi unit they were going to work with, PMT could be tailored to the specifics of the rotation. In these cases, the interviewees spoke most highly of the usefulness of their PMT. Finally, interviewees stated that practicing with interpreters was an important aspect of PMT.[41]

---

[40] Company Grade Officer, Camp Ripley, Afghanistan, February 27, 2013.

[41] A common example was the use of a "reverse interpreter" to prevent mentors who were fluent in Arabic from speaking English directly to the mock partners—who of course were fluent in English. The reverse interpreter technique requires that the Arabic-speaking operator speak Arabic to the interpreter, who then speaks English to the mock force. A related technique for mentors who were not fluent in Arabic was to speak English to the interpreter, who then passed on the instructions in English to the mock partner force.

Summary

The U.S. focus on tactical mentorship of ICTF, in conjunction with early control over recruitment, selection, and equipping, helped yield tactically proficient units that gained early praise in U.S. assessments. Reports from interview sources are mixed in terms of the degree to which U.S. teams focused on building ISOF capability versus achieving operational effects. Some suggest that U.S. Special Forces teams were quick to promote unilateral operations, while others suggest that these teams continued to play a prominent role in tactical operations. What does seem clear is that a U.S. focus on tactical units limited the degree of mentorship available to senior Iraqi commanders and staff, as well as support units critical to independent operations. ISOF logistics capability was slow to mature and possibly hampered by U.S. teams eager to address shortfalls by directly equipping Iraqi units with U.S. materials. The direct provision of intelligence targeting packages also undercut the ability of Iraqi units to learn this critical skill.

As Iraqis took operational control of ISOF, challenges began to emerge regarding the quality of Iraqi officers. Interviews suggest that the Iraqi officer corps of the ICTF may have been troubled from the start, with some junior officers struggling to demonstrate basic combat leadership skills. However, as Iraqis took control of ICTF, problems of nepotism began to take hold, with unqualified individuals assigned to key positions, including the CTC commander. Sectarianism also became evident, with the ICTF increasingly focusing on Sunni targets.

Continuity of operations appeared to benefit most when U.S. units returned to work with the same Iraqi partners. Where this was not the case, there was a tendency for incoming units to begin mentoring from scratch and re-train skills already taught and learned. It appears that PMT was often focused on building direct action rather than mentoring skills. Though some Special Forces teams thought that this focus was appropriate for their mission, other Special Forces and Navy SEAL teams thought that they would have benefited from PMT that focused on the FID aspect of their mission. To this extent, operators reported that the use of a mock partner force, especially one emanating from U.S. Army non-infantry units, was a particularly helpful component of PMT. If the deploying unit knew the identity and details of their upcoming partner force, then PMT (as well as the mock partner force) could be shaped to the specifics of their upcoming deployment.

Postscript: Iraqi SOF Performance in 2014

The crisis in Iraqi security that began in late 2013 in Anbar and then dramatically worsened with the fall of Mosul to extremists in 2014 has created an extraordinary test of ISOF. This test has highlighted both the successes and shortfalls of U.S. partnership with ISOF. While a full assessment of ISOF performance is beyond the scope of this report, some initial observations are possible.

In terms of success, ISOF have fought much better than most Iraqi security forces. In the battle around the critical Bayji oil refinery in June 2014, ISOF bore the brunt of combat. Though eventually driven out of the refinery, ISOF seem to have contested the refinery effectively for days.[42]

At the same time, ISOF seem to have been plagued by the same limits on intelligence and logistics that have hampered the broader Iraqi security forces. Similarly, there are reports that, like other parts of the Iraqi security forces, ISOF have been implicated in the extrajudicial killing of prisoners, often with a sectarian character.[43] While ISOF may not have been involved in these killings, the sectarianism noted before 2014 is unlikely to improve in the near term.

---

[42] Bill Chappell, "Iraq Battles Militants for Key Oil Refinery in Beiji," *NPR*, June 19, 2014.

[43] Ahmed Rasheed and Oliver Holmes, "Prisoner Deaths Indicate Mass Executions by Iraqi Police," *Reuters*, June 27, 2014.

CHAPTER SIX

SOF Partnership in Colombia

The U.S. Army has a long history of military-to-military links with the Colombian Armed Forces. American Army Rangers played a key role in establishing the Lancero training course at Fort Tolemaida in the 1950s, and, since then, there has been an almost continual presence in the country. Perhaps the most intensive engagement, however, was between 1998 and 2006, when U.S. Army Special Forces played a key role in training and assisting partner units in counternarcotics, counterinsurgency, and counterterrorism. These efforts were initially included as part of Plan Colombia, but were subsequently incorporated as a central component of Plan Patriota, the first stage in President Alvaro Uribe's Democratic Security and Defense Policy (Politica de Defense y Seguridad Democratica).

This chapter will examine the U.S. SOF partnership experience in Colombia. It will provide a brief overview of the situation in the country in the late 1990s before outlining the basic tenets of Plan Colombia and Plan Patriota. Following this, a discussion of the main Colombian Armed Forces units that U.S. SOF worked with will be undertaken, paying particular attention to some of the initial obstacles and challenges that had to be overcome. The chapter will then examine how the engagement process worked in terms of force ratios, rotation, and rapport building. It will conclude by looking at main areas in which Colombian SOF improved and some of the main lessons that can be extrapolated from the Colombian experience.

Methodology

This chapter draws on both primary and secondary sources. The primary sources are interviews conducted by RAND analysts with both U.S. and Colombian personnel in March–April 2013.[1] In addition, this chapter draws on the extensive academic, journalistic, and policy research on Colombia.

Colombia in the Late 1990s: Drugs, Insurgency, and Terrorism and the Initiation of Plans Colombia and Patriota

By the late 1990s, Colombia was facing a confluence of threats that were seriously undermining domestic stability, tearing at the national fabric of social cohesion, and challenging the government's monopoly of power. Not only was the country the world's main producer and exporter of cocaine, it was also the locus of protracted left-wing insurgencies stemming from the Fuerzas Armadas Revolucionias de Colombia (FARC) and the smaller Ejército de Liberación Nacional (ELN).[2] Compounding the situation were the activities of paramilitaries that had united under the banner of the Autodefensas Unidas de Colombia (AUC). These militias first emerged in reaction to the activities of FARC and the ELN, predominantly operating in areas where the government was unable to provide security to the population. Over time, however, they systematically degenerated into exceptionally violent criminal entities motivated more or less exclusively by the drug trade.[3]

---

[1]   Due to sensitivities, RAND staff were not able to interview a significant number of personnel currently serving in Colombia.

[2]   Indeed, at the time, the assessment from the U.S. Defense Intelligence Agency was that the Colombian Armed Forces was not only losing ground to FARC but could actually suffer a wholesale defeat within five years. See "Los Militares Estan Perdiendo la Guerra," *El Timepo*, April 23, 1998.

[3]   For an analysis of the various challenges confronting the Colombian state at the turn of the millennium, see Angel Rabasa and Peter Chalk, *Colombian Labyrinth: The Synergy of*

In response to the deteriorating situation, President Andres Pastrana launched Plan Colombia in 1998.[4] Developed with the direct backing of President Bill Clinton and, later, George W. Bush, this broad menu of policy proposals was designed to deal with all aspects of the country's domestic political, social, economic, and military ills. The centerpiece of the initiative was a militarized counternarcotics strategy aimed at achieving "a full-court press on all trafficking organizations and critical nodes to completely disrupt [and] destroy their production and shipping capabilities."[5]

Following September 11, 2001, the Bush administration succeeded in extending the focus of Plan Colombia under the aegis of the war on terrorism. From 2002 to 2006, the Colombian government implemented Plan Patriota, which focused on reestablishing national control over all Colombian municipalities and major tracts of rural territory.[6]

Drugs and Insurgency and Its Implications for Regional Stability, Santa Monica, Calif.: RAND Corporation, MR-1339-AF, 2001.

[4] Plan Colombia was actually a joint initiative among U.S. Special Operations Command, Colombia, and several Latin/Central American states. Its roots date back to 1995–1996, when counternarcotics money first became available to U.S. Special Forces as a deployment tool. In 1996, a Special Operations Command–sponsored conference held in Miami identified Colombia, Peru, Bolivia, and Venezuela as the countries most in need of counternarcotics assistance (informally known as the Andean Ridge Initiative). Of these, it was determined that Colombia was the number-one priority, and, within U.S. Southern Command, an unwritten rule emerged that whatever Bogotá requested it received. Retired member, 7th Special Forces Group (hereafter referred to as 7th SFG), Niceville, April 2013.

[5] Cited in Peter Zirnite, "The Militarization of the Drug War in Latin America," *Current History*, Vol. 97, No. 618, 1998, p. 168. See also Michael Shifter, "Colombia at War," *Current History*, Vol., 98, No. 626, 1999, pp. 120–21.

[6] In August 2006, a second phase of the Democratic Security and Defense Policy commenced—Plan Consolidacion. This aimed to build and entrench trust between the army and the domestic population by systematically handing over reclaimed areas to civilian control and incorporating non-kinetic, "soft" measures that involve all organs of government in the overall counterinsurgency strategy. For further details see German Giraldo Restrepo, *Transforming the Colombian Army During the War on Terrorism*, Carlisle, Pa.: U.S. Army War College, March 2006; Adam Isacson, *Consolidating "Consolidation": Colombia's "Security and Development" Zones Await a Civilian Handoff, While Washington Backs Away from the Concept*, Washington, D.C.: Washington Office on Latin America, December 2012; and Jeremy McDermott, "Destination Victory," *Jane's Intelligence Review*, July 2007, p. 58.

An immediate requirement of Plan Patriota was the need to channel increased resources to the Colombian military. President Uribe achieved this by doubling the defense budget from 2 to 4 percent of gross domestic product. The size of the army was subsequently increased to 60,000 personnel, and five joint commands were created to correspond with the major operational areas of threat groups. To enhance individual effectiveness and professionalism within the army, recruitment was also progressively converted from a draft system to one based on volunteers. Integral to this effort was Plan 10,000, which sought to first replace 30,000 regular soldiers (*solados bachillieres*) with career troops and then increase the rate of transformation by 10,000 per year.[7] Finally, Colombia stepped up the overall tempo of its engagement with the United States to upgrade existing units and create new ones.[8]

Partnership Approach

Units and Task Organization

Between 1998 and 2006, special ODA teams from the U.S. Army's 7th SFG spearheaded American Joint Combined Exchange for Training (JCET) missions in Colombia—although requests for riverine units to patrol the country's 18,000 kilometers of navigable waterways also brought in Navy SEALs during the later stages of this period.[9] The number of U.S. military personnel and civilian contractors allowed in Colombia at any one time was capped at 400 each, and all activity was

[7]   Restrepo, 2006, p. 11; Jeremy McDermott, "Colombia Imposes Democratic Authority," *Jane's Intelligence Review*, October 2002.

[8]   Comments made by a Colombian delegate during the Center for Civil Military Relations' workshop titled "Responses to Maritime Security," Monterey, Calif., Naval Postgraduate School, September 6–10, 2010. See also United States Institute of Peace, *Civil Society Under Siege in Colombia*, Washington, D.C., Special Report 114, February 2004, p. 7.

[9]   Serving member, 7th SFG, Eglin Air Force Base (AFB), April 2013. See also Jeremy McDermott, "Green Berets Move into Colombia," *The Daily Telegraph* (UK), October 12, 1998.

confined to a strict train-and-assist function, with no American forces engaged in actual combat missions.[10]

Between 1999 and 2001, the U.S.-Colombian partnering process was mainly based on establishing the Counter Narcotics Brigade, which over the course of these two years involved 85 American Special Forces trainers, deployed on a permanent basis.[11] After 2001, ODAs typically consisted of 10–12 people and worked with a class of up to 150 men. Ratios would depend on the type of training being given and what resources were available, although it was extremely rare for anything more than a company to be engaged. By the same token, there would occasionally be instances when a U.S. training team would be responsible for just a few cadres, though this generally occurred only when imparting highly specialized niche capabilities.[12]

Mission Focus

The initial purpose of U.S. Special Forces training and partnership in Colombia was to enhance the capabilities of Colombian security forces to crush the critical nodes of cocaine production and trafficking in the country. The American effort centered on supply interdiction and focused on militarizing the police fight against the drug trade through the provision of intelligence, hardware (specifically helicopters),[13] and tactical training.[14]

As noted, the initial thrust was directed to boosting the country's counternarcotics capabilities. U.S. instructors had already been working to establish elite airborne squads in the police—known as Jungle

---

[10] Jeremy McDermott, "USA Faces Colombian Dilemma," *Jane's Intelligence Review*, April 2003, p. 21.

[11] By telephone, retired member, Special Boat Squadron, May 2013.

[12] Serving members, 7th SFG, Eglin AFB; embassy officials, U.S. diplomatic mission, Mexico City, April 2013.

[13] The Colombians currently have more than 200 Blackhawk helicopters, which is the largest such fleet in the world outside the United States.

[14] Officials, U.S. Embassy, Mexico City, April 2013; senior analyst, Control Risks Group, Mexico City, April 2013.

Commandos (or Junglas)—and this effort continued.[15] In addition, the United States worked to create a new dedicated Counter Narcotics Brigade (Brigada Contra el Narcotráfico).[16] Three battalions were eventually established, each with a strength of 980 men.[17]

Following the expansion of Plan Colombia, the remit of the U.S. Special Forces training function was extended to include both counterterrorism and counterinsurgency.[18] The 7th SFG focused on boosting the capabilities of two existing elite forces: the Special Forces Commando Brigade (Brigada de Fuerzas Especiales Commando; BFEC)[19] and a dedicated hostage-rescue squad called Unified Action Groups for Personal Liberty (Grupos de Acción Unificada Libertad Personal; GAULA).[20]

U.S. Special Forces advisors were also instrumental in establishing several new units, including[21]

- Commando Brigade (Brigada Commando; BC), which was trained to conduct short-term jungle operations aimed at neutralizing rebel leaders

---

[15] Anonymous interview, date withheld.

[16] U.S. officials, Mexico City, April 2013. See also Steve Salisbury, "Colombian Crack Troops," *Soldier of Fortune*, April 1999. The Comando Especial del Ejercito (CEE) was a small unit that was trained in both urban and rural combat and had the unique role of carrying out tasks that were traditionally in the domain of the police.

[17] By telephone, retired member, Special Boat Service, May 2013. See also Gabriel Marcella, *The United States and Colombia: The Journey from Ambiguity to Strategic Clarity*, Carlisle, Pa.: U.S. Army War College Strategic Studies Institute, May 2003, p. 9.

[18] Senior analyst, Washington Office on Latin America (hereafter referred to as WOLA), Washington, D.C., March 2013.

[19] By Skype, senior analyst, National Defense University, Washington, D.C., March 2013.

[20] GAULA forces are split between military and police units. The former are responsible for rural operations, the latter for urban missions. Serving GAULA members, Bogotá and Cali, Colombia, September 2001.

[21] Plan Patriota also included other adjustments to the Colombian police and security forces, though these did not directly involve U.S. Special Forces personnel. See Thomas A. Marks, *Sustainability of Colombian Military/Strategic Support for "Democratic Security,"* Carlisle, Pa.: U.S. Army War College Strategic Studies Institute, July 2005, pp. 11–12; and "Interview: General Martin Carreno," *Jane's Intelligence Review*, March 2004, p. 58.

- Rapid Deployment Force (La Fuerza de Despliegue Rápido; FUDRA), which was integrated into the Special Forces Commando Brigade to operate in jungle, prairie, desert, and high-altitude environments and attack the structure and leadership of terrorist groups
- Aviation Brigade (Brigada Aviación; BA), which was tasked with providing air support to the Jungle Commandos and Colombian Armed Forces[22]
- Urban Counter-Terrorism Special Forces Group (Agrupación de Fuerzas Especiales Antiterroristas Urbanas; AFEUR), which was exclusively trained by the 7th SFG's Charlie Group and has since emerged as the tier-one unit in the Colombian Armed Forces.[23]

When the Colombian government requested assistance for a unit, an ODA would be deployed to conduct a PDSS. This assessment was used to determine the baseline abilities of the subjects to be taught, the location of appropriate training locations, the number of instructors required, how long the engagement should last, what should be included in the program of instruction, and what equipment was needed (mission critical, mission essential, and mission enhanced). JCETs would be unit (rather than individual) based and typically lasted 45 days, although they could go on for as long as two to three months, depending on the type of skills to be imparted.

The specific makeup of the program of instruction would vary according to the training mission at hand. However, most included a combination of components that focused on leadership qualities (especially at the non-officer level), rules of engagement, communications, navigation, escape and evasion, fire and maneuver, intelligence, military medicine, marksmanship (both flat-range and close-quarter battle), and field training exercises.[24]

---

[22] The Aviation Brigade accounts for the bulk of monetary training assistance that the United States has given Colombia.

[23] Senior analyst, WOLA, Washington, D.C., March 2013. See also Restrepo, 2006, pp. 9–12.

[24] Serving members, 7th SFG, Eglin AFB, April 2013.

While American ODAs engaged with individual Colombian SOF units, the intent was always that these units would work closely with general-purpose forces. Integration of this sort—which followed the same pattern as American train-and-assist missions in Iraq and Afghanistan—was deemed essential to ensuring the effective execution of large-scale operations where full interoperability between specialist teams and standard army regiments was critical. It was also regarded as necessary for reducing intelligence stovepiping and providing a logical career chain from conventional to nonconventional forces.[25]

As the parameters of Plan Colombia expanded, so too did the goals of Washington's advise-and-assist mission. The immediate priority was to achieve a series of rapid victories against threat groups to boost troop morale. Support was thus directed at improving the ability (and willingness) of troops to operate away from base and forward deploy to the heart of enemy-controlled zones. The objective in the words of one commentator was "to hit FARC, the ELN, and AUC as hard as possible, as quickly as possible, and as cheaply as possible."[26]

Once Plan Patriota came on line under the Uribe administration, the U.S./Colombian aim changed to restoring public confidence in the capacity of Colombian Armed Forces to seize and hold areas that were either contested or fully beyond government control. Defensive and offensive operations that targeted rebel leaders (decapitation strikes), destroyed guerrilla infrastructure, and reinforced legitimacy and popular backing for the counterinsurgency campaign were all regarded as key, as was an emphasis on mobility, speed, and flexibility.[27]

Over the longer term, the goal of American trainers was to ensure that the Colombians were fully self-sufficient. The ultimate aim was the creation of a professional indigenous SOF community that could not only operate independently but, ideally, also play a key role in offset-

---

[25] Officials, U.S. Embassy, Mexico City, April 2013.

[26] By Skype, senior analyst, National Defense University, Washington, D.C., March 2013.

[27] Restrepo, 2006, p. 14.

ting the U.S. training burden in Latin America by acting as a regional exporter of good practices.[28]

Rapport

U.S. instructors placed considerable emphasis on building rapport with the Colombian troops to which they were assigned, as this was deemed the most effective way to establish close working relationships, trust, and, crucially, loyalty. Language familiarity was extremely useful in this regard, allowing for direct communication as well as providing a common conduit for sharing stories and life experiences. Beyond this, American trainers would ensure that they fully integrated with their students—they ate the same food, lived in the same quarters (as opposed to hotels), joined in the same recreational activities, and participated in the same physical training routines.[29]

Specific techniques were also used to foster rapport. One was to constantly reinforce successes by verbally acknowledging exercises and drills that were done well—on both an individual and group level. Another was to take the time to see what an individual required and then to provide the item(s) without being asked. Most significantly, instructors took pains to always treat counterparts with full respect, stressing that they had a considerable amount to offer in terms of enriching partnerships, not least by imparting knowledge and skills that were directly relevant to the Colombian theater.[30]

U.S. personnel were also able to leverage certain strengths and advantages that made the entire partnering exercise simpler. One major facet was the recognition on the Colombian side that they not only needed help but that the United States was a logical choice for rendering assistance, given the long history of military ties between the two countries.[31] This prior working experience had the additional benefit

---

[28] Officials, U.S. Embassy, Mexico City, April 2013.

[29] Serving members, 7th SFG, Eglin AFB, Niceville, and Mexico City, April 2013.

[30] Serving members, 7th SFG, Eglin AFB, April 2013. As one officer candidly remarked, "If you treat them like bums, they will end up as bums."

[31] Serving members, 7th SFG, Eglin AFB, April 2013; officials, U.S. Embassy, Mexico City, April 2013.

of allowing American instructors to reasonably ascertain the baseline capability of Colombian Armed Forces—which is often one of the largest obstacles confronting a SOF training mission.[32]

An equally significant factor was the nationalistic and proud nature of the Colombians. Soldiers were physically and mentally tough, wanted to learn, were eager to engage, would not give up, and above all yearned to be the best.[33] This attitude is perhaps best reflected in the rigorous manner in which the Colombian Armed Forces prepare for the annual South Fuerzas Commando. The event, which is organized by the United States and involves SOF units from across South America pitting their skills against one another, is routinely won by the Colombian Urban Counter-Terrorism Special Forces Group, which will typically devote months of training to prepare for the competition.[34]

Finally, there were no major linguistic barriers between the Americans and Colombians. A significant number of the 7th SFG are fluent in Spanish, and all members of an ODA would be required to converse in the language for at least a month prior to deployment as part of their PMT. Being able to communicate in the local dialect not only precluded the need for interpreters (which, as Afghanistan and Iraq have demonstrated, can pose risks to operational security, as there is no way to know exactly what is being translated), it also naturally allowed empathy and trust to build up between trainer and trainee.[35]

---

[32] Anonymous interview, date withheld.

[33] Serving members, 7th SFG, Eglin AFB, April 2013; officials, U.S. Embassy, Mexico City, April 2013; senior analyst, Control Risks Group, Mexico City, April 2013.

[34] Serving members, 7th SFG, Eglin AFB, April 2013; senior analyst, WOLA, Washington, D.C., March 2013. It should be noted that one officer with the 7th SFG saw this as more of a weakness and reflective of a somewhat dysfunctional machismo mindset. This is because while the competition is primarily meant to be an exercise to promote military-to-military ties and build partnership and trust, the Colombians merely see it as an opportunity to demonstrate their superiority.

[35] Serving members, 7th SFG, Eglin AFB, April 2013.

Key Partnering Tasks
Logistics

Logistics were a major challenge, as the logistical chain was highly underdeveloped, frequently leaving troops without the necessary resources to operate for sustained periods on the ground.[36] Antiquated and/or faulty equipment was another major issue; ammunition was corroded; night-vision goggles had no protective eye shields;[37] and there was a dearth of even basic supplies, such as cleaning rags and gun oil. Colombian Armed Forces would often ask for equipment based on its cache, rather than relevance to a particular mission statement.[38]

The overall procedure for requesting U.S. support was also inefficient, as the mechanisms for requesting assistance were extremely haphazard, especially in terms of determining what type of training was required, which units needed to be engaged, and where instruction should take place. As a result of personnel changes in the American-Colombia military group, the process of applying for assistance was improved by requiring all training requests to be lodged at least 60 days in advance and in accordance with a well-thought-out strategic plan of what the end state should be. This provided ODAs with sufficient time and "vision" to undertake comprehensive PDSSs and assess appropriate training needs and equipment requirements.[39]

Intelligence

Initially, the Colombian Armed Forces were devoid of an indigenous intelligence capacity and heavily dependent on information fed from

---

[36] Serving members, 7th SFG, Eglin AFB, April 2013.

[37] Serving members, 7th SFG, Eglin AFB, April 2013. Several of these interviewees remarked that this deficiency made Colombians highly reluctant to undertake night patrols due to the fear that the glow from the night-vision goggles would make them a target for a sniper.

[38] On this point, one member of the 7th SFG remarked, "The Colombians wanted to be the best, but there was a lot of Hollywood involved. They wanted all the 'toys'—the cool stuff, irrespective of its operational value."

[39] Retired member, 7th SFG, Niceville, April 2013. According to this interviewee, the appointment of Colonel Kevin Higgins was particularly pertinent to streamlining the overall assistance request process.

the police. However, with U.S. assistance, the government also invested heavily in both augmenting Colombian intelligence capacity and ensuring there was a more streamlined two-way street for disseminating real-time operational information between military and nonmilitary units.[40] By 2004, three precise, intelligence-led missions helped turn the tide against the insurgency. These operations ("Liberty," "Marital," and "Jorga Mara") helped to significantly reduce the strength of six major FARC fronts by destroying more than 356 combat camps, eliminating much of the group's leadership, and effectively neutralizing strategically important guerrilla rearguard areas in the southern provinces of Meta, Guaviare, and Caqueta (where most of the country's cocaine production is concentrated).[41]

Operational Planning

Operational planning was another challenge, for many reasons. First, a significant proportion—more than three-quarters—of Colombian security units were made up of conscripts, meaning that the quality and morale of troops was typically low (as they simply did not want to be there).[42] The army was a "garrison force" and would frequently fail to engage the enemy on its own turf. Soldiers were highly officer-oriented and incapable of thinking on their feet or thinking "outside the box." The military lacked a proficient NCO cadre—often seen as the backbone of an effective fighting force. Illiteracy was rife, and criminal corruption, although not endemic, was certainly present, particularly among conscripts.[43]

---

[40] According to one interviewee, this change was primarily driven by Colombian Armed Forces' desire to mimic how the intelligence cycle works in the United States.

[41] "Interview: General Martin Carreno," 2004, p. 58; Marks, 2005, p. 14; Jeremy McDermott, "Colombian Insurgency Escalates as Guerrillas Go Back on Offensive," *Jane's Intelligence Review*, July 2005, p. 9.

[42] Thomas Marks, "Colombian Crossroads," *Soldier of Fortune*, September 2001, p. 60. According to one contractor, conscripts were generally "trapped" into serving, which further undermined their morale and motivation.

[43] Senior analyst, WOLA, Washington, D.C., March 2013, and Eglin AFB, Niceville, and Mexico City, April 2013.

To an extent, some of these problems were ameliorated through policy changes instituted in Bogotá and Washington. For instance, an integral part of Plan Patriota was devoted to systematically transforming the Colombian Armed Forces into a largely professional force. Today, about 70 percent of the army's SOF personnel are career soldiers.[44] Corruption was effectively dealt with through increased vetting procedures for senior commanders and higher salaries.[45]

As far as possible, repeat JCETs to the same location would be undertaken to build on the training conducted previously. In these instances, the mission would typically not commence where the previous one left off—rather stepping instruction down a layer to ensure that the handover was comprehensive. While not particularly cost-effective (in that certain modules would be repeated), it did ensure that there were no gaps and that all learning blocs had been fully completed.[46]

Summary

U.S. engagement with the Colombian Armed Forces between 1998 and 2007 was highly successful. Improvements were witnessed across the board, from operational planning to institutional organization. By the end of this period, Colombian units were motivated and actively engaging the enemy not only in their own territory but also in safe havens outside the country. Soldiers were following strict codes of conduct, exhibiting acute discipline in the moderated use of violence. Also, the former static, officer-centric mold of the army—something that is common to most Latin American militaries—had been eliminated and replaced with one that not only centered around a proactive NCO cadre but also emphasized (and rewarded) innovative thinking.[47]

---

[44] Serving members, 7th SFG, Eglin AFB, April 2013.

[45] Officials, U.S. Embassy, Mexico City, April 2013.

[46] Serving members, 7th SFG, Eglin AFB, April 2013.

[47] Serving members, 7th SFG, Eglin AFB, April 2013; officials, U.S. Embassy, Mexico City, April 2013. The 2013 report on Colombia by Human Rights Watch at least partially corroborates the interviews, noting that "[t]here has been a dramatic reduction in cases of alleged

Finally, Colombian SOF units were playing an increasingly active role in training partner units located in other Latin and Central American states. By 2006, the Jungle Commandos were training counterparts from Panama, Costa Rico, Belize, Mexico, Argentina, Paraguay, Peru, and the Dominican Republic. An elite helicopter school established at Melgar, Tolemaida—which is modeled after a similar facility at Fort Rucker in the United States—was also regularly hosting combat aviators from Ecuador, Peru, and Mexico to hone close-quarter flight insertion and extraction skills.[48]

Several lessons can be drawn from the American experience in Colombia. First, engagement is far easier if there is a history of military-to-military ties and no major linguistic barriers. Second, the ability to impart training very much depends on buy-in from the host nation—the willingness to not only accept assistance but also internalize and build on it. Third, engagements are far easier when they involve career-oriented professional soldiers as opposed to conscripts. Fourth, establishing a viable NCO cadre is extremely important for building a force contingent that is adaptable and capable of innovative, proactive thinking. Fifth, rapport is indispensable to fostering trust, solidarity, and long-term relationships. Sixth, SOF operations should not be considered in isolation but, rather, as a subset of a larger military strategy that combines and integrates specialized units with general-purpose forces.

---

extrajudicial killings attributed to the security forces since 2009; nevertheless, some cases were reported in 2011 and 2012." See Human Rights Watch, "Colombia," in *World Report 2013*, 2013.

[48] Officials, U.S. Embassy, Mexico City, April 2013. See also "Colombia Trains Mexico Pilots," *Diáglo*, January 1, 2013.

CHAPTER SEVEN

Best Practices and Recommendations for SOF Partnering

This chapter is based on a review of best practices and challenges from the previous chapters on Afghanistan, Iraq, and Colombia. It makes recommendations oriented around three main categories of challenges and best practices: OPTEMPO and sustainability; depth of partnership and rapport; and continuity and training. Some of these recommendations may not be implementable in the present circumstances in Afghanistan, but may be possible post-2014. They are also intended to be useful in future SOF capacity-building missions.

Operational Tempo and Sustainability

Operations Must Be Subordinated to Capability Development

A focus on achieving operational effects with Afghan partner forces has superseded the development of Afghan SOF capability across nearly all the special operations units visited as part of this study. A frequent refrain across interviews was that Afghan SOF are tactically proficient, but they do not have the structures necessary for operational planning, intelligence collection, logistics, etc. To create operational effects, coalition partner units must provide these enabling functions, further stunting their development within Afghan SOF. This vicious circle was particularly pronounced within the Commando companies of the SOKs, as U.S. SOF units frequently conducted complex clearance operations with the *kandaks*. The danger is that such operations are not sustainable by the Afghans, they overburden the retention capabilities of the individual Afghan soldiers, they leave limited time for training, and they consume much of the ODA's time while planning for operations.

Some coalition partner units, though, have lately shifted focus to building unit capability. The British forces mentoring CF 333 were focusing on training and mentorship and promoting independent Afghan operations. Part of promoting an independent Afghan SOF capability has been limiting direct support assets for the Afghans, such as operational UAV feeds, and limiting the degree to which the British forces provision the Afghans with coalition intelligence. The MOI requirement to move to warrant-based operations played a critical role in this transition. Of course, by decreasing OPTEMPO and increasing reliance on Afghan intelligence, the British recognized that such an approach reduced their direct impact on the insurgency in the short term. However, they felt this was necessary if they were to effectively build unit skills and prepare the Afghans for subsequent transition. As noted, the result has been a drop in OPTEMPO, but at least some NMUs were able to function using primarily Afghan intelligence.

The U.S./Romanian teams partnered with a PRC in Kapisa initially assumed operations with a command intent of targeting Joint Prioritized Engagement Lists. However, a serious operational mishap on the part of the PRC required the unit to cease high-risk arrest operations, which in turn paved the way for a slower pace of operations. During the stand-down, the mentors focused the PRC on conducting simple dismounted patrols, which allowed the mentors to help the PRC focus on simple but key tasks, such as routinely wearing their night-vision goggles and conducting tactically proficient dismounted patrols.

The same problems of focusing on operations rather than building capacity were also evident in Iraq. ICTF and other ISOF were very good as individual soldiers and were tactically proficient as small units. However, leadership and independent capability to plan and sustain operations remained relatively stunted. While these units continued to function after the withdrawal of most U.S. personnel from Iraq, recent reports—particularly the fighting in 2014—suggest that, combined with ongoing politicization of the force, this lack of fully developed leadership and independent capability has hampered the force.

As the United States and international community continue to work toward building sustainable Afghan SOF capability as well as the capability of other partner SOF outfits, there should be a focus on conducting smaller and less complex operations that can inculcate partner-unit confidence and permit failure without catastrophic results. Assuming indigenous air assets will be limited—as they are in Afghanistan— then, where possible, partner SOF units should conduct simpler and more local ground assault operations over air operations. They should also conduct training exercises that give the SOF partners experience working complex operations. Simpler operations would also enable the partner elements to practice intelligence-operations integration and would allow the partner commanders the opportunity to practice creating their own operational plans. Obviously, as partner capabilities increase, so can the complexity of operations. To sustain such an effort will require a clear commander's intent. It will also require partner units to be evaluated on improvements in capacity, instead of on operations or simple kill/capture numbers.

In future campaigns, these efforts to build operational capacity should be initiated in the early stages of partnership rather than later. The U.S. and coalition focus on building partner capability (rather than as a simple face for coalition operations) started late in both the Iraq and Afghan campaigns. In both cases the result has been underdevelopment of key capabilities.

Such a focus on building partner capacity vice exerting operational effects will confront a significant hurdle in any campaign where American and coalition lives are at risk. In Afghanistan, exposed VSO sites and the overarching campaign against the Taliban created a natural demand for operations that could broaden security zones. As illustrated in our interviews, focusing on partner capacity building can limit the type and tempo of operations that would most significantly affect an insurgency. The British, for example, have recognized this sacrifice and readily note that their focus on training has in turn limited the degree to which they have been able to affect the insurgency. It is our view that while commanders must ultimately weigh the appropriate balance, they should ensure that partnered forces must develop the skills and institutional capacity to continue security operations after U.S. and allied forces depart the theater of operations.

Focus on Sustainable Operations

Given the time-limited nature of most capacity-building efforts, it is increasingly important for SOF mentors to focus on promoting sustainable operations. As is the case in Afghanistan, many coalition assets, such as rotary-wing air and direct ISR support, provided to Afghan units will fade quickly. A best practice that emerged from our interviews is the need to consider the Afghan capability to replace coalition enablers and to account for this in present-day operations. For example, the British forces mentoring CF 333 began to ask what resources the Afghans will have access to post-withdrawal, and planned to provide only those resources until then. We know, for example, that Afghans will not have UAVs. Though UAV overwatch is important when coalition forces are exposed during operations, the British did not provide this capability to Afghan commanders.

The "shadow of withdrawal" also affected the Lithuanian approach to PRC mentorship, as they were also trying to get the Afghans to use their own sources of intelligence and equipment. ISR was an enabler but was being minimized to wean the Afghans away from assets they will not have after coalition withdrawal. In some ways, the Lithuanian mentors were more prepared for this approach than most coalition forces, because they often lacked the resources and assets of their wealthier coalition counterparts. They lacked certain intelligence collection capabilities because they are not in the "Five Eyes" community, but this was taken as a positive since it was not another asset that would be taken away post-2014.

ISOF in Iraq also lacked a substantial SIGINT capability. While this limited overall unit capability, it also meant that the loss of U.S. SIGINT was not catastrophic. One recent assessment of ISOF noted that because the Iraqis rely less on mobile-phone tracking and similar techniques, the loss of coalition resources to perform such techniques will not affect the Iraqi SOF much.

In light of such lessons, it will be important for mentor units, in Afghanistan and beyond, to carefully consider the anticipated level

Box 7.1. Use Tabletop Exercises to Enhance Coordination and Planning

In an attempt to help Afghan officers plan for the loss of aerial MEDEVAC, the British forces mentoring CF 333 planned a table-top exercise for ground MEDEVAC assets. Realizing that this was principally a command and control problem, one mentor said, "Afghans don't empower subordinates and they rarely seek their advice and counsel. We brought key Afghan players together, such as signals, medics, and [the operations officer]. . . . We wanted [the operations officer] to understand that he can't do everything." Once that breakthrough had been achieved in a low-pressure situation, not only were the personnel better prepared to plan for ground casualty evacuations and other contingencies, but delegation of all operations improved. As an Afghan operations officer recounted, "This is a really good lesson for us. [We] learned that we need to involve everyone in planning and we will do this in the future."

of indigenous force assets and incorporate these considerations into operational planning. For example, the lack of Afghan air capacity is one major limitation noted throughout our interviews. Coalition forces should consequently prioritize ground assault forces over helicopter assault forces in both training and operations. As the examples above suggest, a similar approach should also be taken for relevant ISR assets. Beginning with the end state in mind and limiting provisioned assets to only those that can be sustained will help avoid challenges that ensue when partnered units must be weaned from coalition enablers.

Deliberately Wean Partner SOF from Unsustainable Support

Many Afghan commanders interviewed for this study spoke with pal-pable fear on the issue of coalition force withdrawal. Virtually all of them feared the loss of critical enabler assets provided by the coalition, such as rotary-wing transport, MEDEVAC, and ISR. Others expressed concern about conducting operations without the presence of coalition mentors. Several commanders reported plans to quit once the mentors withdraw.

A major source of concern is that many of these Afghan officers have received little guidance on the phasing of the drawdown of mentorship assets. This was no doubt a result of the strategic context, as such decisions had not yet been made. However, without this guidance, fears run wild that support will be removed "cold turkey." Such rapid and ad hoc reduction in support could not only undermine unit cohesion and morale but also deal a fatal blow to operational capacity, as Afghan SOF would not have time to adjust to the lower level of support.

Mentorship of partner units, as well as enabling assets, should be withdrawn slowly and phased out over time. British forces mentoring ATF 444, along with other coalition units, have begun to tell their Afghan counterparts that there is no more money. They are also starting to force a shift to Afghan logistics systems. The former CJSOTF-A commander has recognized this necessity. At the conclusion of his command tenure, he urged an end to the dependence on coalition enablers and says the Commandos have to learn to do without coalition MEDEVAC, close air support, and sustainment. Of course, such an approach will result in a near-term reduction in Afghan capability.

The number and size of mentor units working with local SOF should also be slowly reduced over time. In Afghanistan, some units,

Box 7.2. Hold a Demonstration

Just as in the U.S. military, demonstrations for key political and military figures in the Afghan government were important. In one case, parliamentarians observed a crisis response in Kabul from a rooftop a safe distance outside the cordon. When officials observe special operations units, they understand the capabilities more clearly and take pride in the unit's success. This can improve supply and logistics and reduce pressure for patronage-based appointments. As one Afghan officer from CF 333 noted, "Many generals and ministers and ambassadors, they are happy to come and see the force. . . . Everyone can see [our force is] at the top. Many people from Parliament, many from your side and our side, come to see the facility we have."

such as CRU and CF 333, have already benefited from the ability to execute unilateral operations or operations with as few as two to four coalition mentors. The British forces mentoring CF 333 have also begun executing plans for phased reductions in force size.

What is more, U.S. and allied mentors should clearly communicate with indigenous SOF partners as to how mentorship and support will be withdrawn over time. This will allow local forces the opportunity to plan accordingly, will avoid fears of a dramatic reduction in support, and will limit the risks of a future rise in attrition, which is a key threat now confronting Afghan SOF. Heeding such advice will require strategic decisionmakers to carefully plan force reductions and communicate such plans to tactical mentor units.

Link SOF to Existing Intelligence Infrastructure

Intelligence is the lynchpin of special operations capability. In the case of the Afghan Commandos, the limited intelligence collection capability meant that the units were reliant on U.S. intelligence. This led U.S. special operations teams to develop operational targets and then craft operational plans. This can create a vicious cycle, as the Commando drive to develop intelligence inputs is undercut and ability to train operational planning impeded. Such problems have historically hampered other Afghan SOF units as well.

In Iraq, U.S. provision of targeting packages that required little ISOF analysis limited the Iraqi ability to turn information into intelligence and integrate such intelligence into operations. In addition, the ability of Iraqi SOF to collect, analyze, and execute actionable intelligence has reportedly deteriorated since the United States pulled its forces from Iraq at the end of 2011. The same reporting indicates that the United States has had to reengage with CTS to assist with intelligence activities. This illustrates that even tactically proficient forces can suffer after the withdrawal of U.S. and allied intelligence support if a concerted effort to build host-nation intelligence capabilities is not made. In 2014, U.S. SOF were recommitted to Iraq to further ameliorate intelligence shortfalls.[1]

---

[1]   Adam Entous, Julian Barnes, and Siobhan Gorman, "CIA Ramps Up Role in Iraq," *Wall Street Journal*, March 11, 2013.

Box 7.3. "Welcome to your Death Star"

In the past, responding to spectacular attacks in Kabul involved a number of senior officers engaging in inappropriate and tactical roles, with some even attempting to "chuck grenades in a fight." In an effort to manage command and control, mentors have developed a common response framework that defines appropriate roles for senior officers. The Death Star quote above refers jokingly to the creation of a command center for the Kabul chief of police, in the hopes of creating a more hands-off role for him. The new model is based on the British "gold, silver, bronze" concept for command and control. Bronze commanders control the immediate cordon around an incident, and there may be numerous bronze commanders in any large-scale response. The gold commander is the most-senior officer in charge of the incident. In the British model, there is a silver commander for every two to three bronze commanders, whose job is to push resources inside the cordon. The Afghans have modified this, preferring a silver commander for every bronze. Having altered it to suit them, the model appears to be catching on, and could be the basis for other incident response systems in other areas.

To address this shortfall in organic Afghan SOF intelligence, a number of coalition mentor units have sought to help connect SOF units to existing Afghan intelligence capabilities. The British forces mentoring CF 333, for example, have sought to help connect CF 333 operational planners and intelligence officers across the broad spectrum of the Afghan intelligence community. The British intelligence mentor, for example, takes both the Afghan operational officer and J-2 with him to Kabul so that they can help foster connections with NTEC and help mentor NTEC on the request for information process. The goal is to improve the quality of NTEC-derived targeting packages. The British have also fostered the creation of weekly targeting meetings that are held with CF 333, GDPSU, the NDS, and NTEC. They have biweekly meetings with the provincial-level *shura* and special investigate units and monthly meetings with provincial NDS officials.

The U.S. Navy SEAL platoon mentoring the 8th SOK has also begun to foster such connections. The 8th SOK has exchanged liaison officers with the ANA's 4th Brigade, and the SEAL team is attempting to work 8th SOK connections with the NDS. These efforts are nascent but promising, particularly given the good relations among the PCOP, Australian SOF and their PRC partners, and the SEALs.

The benefits of building a SOF intelligence capability were especially highlighted in Colombia, where the Colombian forces were initially devoid of intelligence capacity. Heavy U.S. and Colombian investment in intelligence capacity helped improve intelligence sharing between military and nonmilitary units. This in turn led to key operational victories against FARC units. This demonstrates that it is not impossible to build such capacity in host-nation SOF, though it takes substantial time and commitment.

Fostering these types of connections will be critically important in post-2014 Afghanistan, as well as future SOF partnerships. First, it will be important to build SOF intelligence collection and analytic capabilities early in the mentoring process. Second, the U.S. and its allies should promote intelligence sharing across indigenous SOF, general-purpose forces, and interagency partners. In Afghanistan, for example, this means U.S. senior leaders should help Afghans understand the importance of developing an MOD-MOI intelligence-sharing agreement. At the tactical and operational level, mentors should help foster connections between partner units and existent intelligence assets. At the most basic level, this will help to foster interoperability and relationships between different SOF units, general-purpose force units, and interagency partners. It will further require promoting the use of liaison officers and joint and interagency synchronization meetings.

Depth of Partnership and Rapport

Promote Deep Partnership Through Extensive Rapport Building

Virtually every individual interviewed as part of this report noted that rapport was the critical ingredient to partnership success. Overall, positive rapport with a partner unit achieves at least two critical objectives.

First, it enhances the effectiveness of training. As one Lithuanian officer remarked, "Being a good friend can allow a mentor to push harder without causing offense." Another similarly stated that positive relationships were key to effective influence. Conversely, poor rapport can hinder effective training: For example, one ODA team reported that their predecessors suffered poor relationships with their Afghan unit and were eventually barred by the *kandak* from working with Afghans on the range.

Second, rapport also seems to offer a dramatic benefit to force protection. At least one unit had such positive relationships with Afghans that they no longer felt it was necessary to carry a personal weapon to the range, and other units told us they did not feel the need to follow the ISAF "guardian angel" requirement of having at least one person in every group interacting with Afghans outside a coalition base carrying a weapon and providing overwatch.

Repeat Deployments Foster Rapport

There are at least seven key factors that help promote positive rapport with partner units. First, units that return time and time again to work with the same partner unit report unusually positive rapport. The Lithuanians, British, and Norwegians have maintained institutional relationships with their partner units and have cycled the same teams to the same locations for a number of years. Afghans frequently remember the names of repeat mentors and voice excitement at their return.

The Value of Non-Transactional Relationships

Second, rapport benefits when mentors engage in non-transactional relationships with Afghans. This was most frequently expressed as "hanging out," including sharing stories, playing sports together, and participating in customs such as sharing tea. Some go even further, taking a cue from the social mores of the Afghans. Lithuanians mentioned that they hold hands with Afghans, while the Norwegians reported that they danced with Afghans as part of a ceremony commemorating the start of the Afghan leave cycle. The British and CF 333 share both Christmas and Eid meals with one another.

Respect Local Culture

Third, respect for Afghan culture is critical and was emphasized by a number of Afghan commanders interviewed for this report. Part of this cultural respect means a nondirective approach to training (see Box 7.4). Beyond this, following appropriate "dos and don'ts" and showing respect for religious customs and mores is critical. Interviewees suggested that Afghans are more than willing to assist in this endeavor, educating the mentors about their religion, culture, and the local situation.

Set a Clear Commander's Intent on Rapport

Fourth, commanders must set a clear intent among subordinates on the need for and importance of rapport. We draw this lesson from the intent provided by the U.S. ODA working with PRC Kapisa. This commander issued four rules that were to guide the treatment of Afghans. One of his subordinates recalled the intent as follows:

> You will treat all the Afghanis with respect; you will not lay hands on them unless [in an] emergency. You will reward them and congratulate them on the things they do well. You will show them that you care. It rolls up to treating them with professional courtesy and treating them with respect.

Box 7.4. Take a Nondirective Approach

Working "by, with, and through" in a mentoring program means offering suggestions rather than giving directions, and saving criticisms for private conversation. It was noted that some U.S. conventional forces train Afghans in the same manner in which they had been trained themselves: "With lots of screaming and sweating at trainees." A Lithuanian officer noted, "This is not the most effective means to get the desired outcomes." A British NCO mentor agreed, saying, "Use a soft approach of suggestion. . . . Those who have an attitude of, 'I am a Westerner, I am here to help you, you will listen to me,' have a harder time."

Train Partner Senior Leaders at Coalition Military Schools

At visits to CF 333, RAND analysts were struck at the degree to which the British have sought to send CF 333 commanders to the Royal Military Academy Sandhurst for formal military schooling. The current CF 333 commander received an education at Sandhurst, as well as several past commanders. This education helped these commanders improve their English-language skills, enhanced their understanding of British military tactics, and surely helped them become more effective leaders. It also enhanced the bond of rapport between these commanders and their British mentors. International Military Education and Training is the U.S. formal program for foreign officer education. Foreign officers and NCOs are invited to attend U.S. military schools and training programs, such as the U.S. Army War College or even the Special Forces Qualification Course. The program seeks to enhance foreign leadership skills, expose leaders to U.S. democratic and human rights values, and promote enhanced military-to-military relationships. In sum, we urge that such programs be utilized to their full extent. In places such as Afghanistan, where the demand for ongoing operations has been high, there is a requirement for U.S. and allied mentors to take a long view of partner-force development. Losing a key operational commander to home-station education represents a short-term loss in capability but one with the potential for long-term gain.

Enhance Language Skills

An important lesson from U.S. assistance to Iraq and Colombia is the value of fostering SOF language skills. Mentors who served in Iraq found that even basic Arabic-language skills helped foster rapport and goodwill with Iraqi special operators. Language was an especially important factor in Colombia. The 7th SFG is primarily dedicated to operating in Central and South America, where Spanish is the most commonly spoken language. Many Special Forces soldiers thus learn Spanish, and many Latin American Special Forces soldiers are drawn to working in the 7th SFG. Familiarity with the Spanish language allows U.S. mentors the opportunity to speak directly to partner forces and helps enhance rapport through shared stories and life experiences. In Afghanistan, it seemed that relatively few U.S. and coalition mentors knew even basic Dari or Pashto. This seemed surprising, given that the war is in its 12th year. Regardless, efforts to enhance relevant host-country language skills among SOF mentors would seem to pay significant benefits to both rapport and training efforts.

Where Possible, Live Together

The degree to which U.S. and allied mentors live in close proximity to host-nation partner forces seems to offer important rapport benefits. In Colombia, American trainers often lived in the same or adja-

---

Box 7.5. Train Together, Fight Together

In a common approach to mentorship, SOF teams often paired one or two mentors to work with Afghans throughout the training and operational cycles. The U.S. ODA working with 1st SOK assigned two SOF soldiers to each company and worked with them during training and then fought side by side during operations. At CF 333, the British color sergeants were assigned mentorship responsibilities to each squadron. In both cases, mentors attested to the value of such an approach. At CF 333, the counterterrorism squadron mentor noted that even at the close of World War II, with the Germans being worn down for manpower, "they never gave up the system where trainers did combat with the German units. We are running that system." He noted that such an approach breeds strong bonds between trainers and Afghan soldiers and limits the risk of green-on-blue incidents: "This fosters the bond; they train and fight together." The mentors at 1st SOK agreed and noted that the trainer-soldier bond pays huge dividends during combat operations. They made a point of putting primary mentors with each of the elements that are most likely to make contact with the enemy:

> When we take casualties, we have had more interface and we know which leaders are strong and which are not. A lot is based on relationships. I have good relationships with most of the platoon sergeants, and that pays huge dividends. We have taken casualties before and communicate with the guys and calm them down and get done what we need to get done.

cent quarters and they ate the same food and enjoyed the same recreational facilities. Norwegian, British, and some U.S. mentors lived in adjoining compounds and close to their Afghan counterparts. Such arrangements facilitated formal mentorship, increased the number of day-to-day interactions, and increased the likelihood of sharing meals. Such close living arrangements of course demand a prerequisite level of trust between partner units. Genuine threats of insider attacks demand greater separation and force-protection measures. Where possible, however, mentors should seek to live as close as possible and even amid the units they seek to train.

Use Mentorship Networks and the Chain of Command to Your Benefit

Logistics is a perennial problem among indigenous SOF units trained by U.S. special operators. In Afghanistan, a commonly referenced story was a unit logistics officer sending resupply requests to higher channels in the MOI or ANASOC only to never receive the requested materials, sometimes not even a confirmation that the request was received. Initially, it was common practice for coalition forces to address this problem by provisioning the Afghans with their own supplies. To address this problem, several units were able to effectively exploit their own mentorship networks that span the Afghan unit's chains of command. For example, the mentors for PRC Kapisa insist that the PRC S-4 submits requests up his chain of command. When they do, the mentor submits the same request through his channels. This allows mentors at higher headquarters or adjacent units to mentor across the Afghan logistics architecture. The LTT outfit at 1st SOK also mastered this technique. They worked through the extensive network of LTT mentors that operate throughout the ANASOC chain of command. In essence, the key is to use the full range of coalition network to address challenges confronting tactical operational units. To achieve this, it is important for mentors to build relationships with higher headquarters staff and personnel from adjacent units so that such relationships can be leveraged when needed.

Assign Senior and Experienced Individuals to Key Mentorship Positions

Effective mentorship often requires assigning appropriately experienced individuals to key mentorship positions. As an example, when the British were deciding to build a special squadron for CF 333, they brought in a uniformed subject-matter expert on a PDSS assignment to develop the training program. The mentor had more than a decade of experience and had the special responsibility of being the home-station instructor. After he submitted his training plan, British headquarters asked him to return to Afghanistan to serve as the squadron's primary mentor. The command then prioritized the squadron by sending the mentor's own sergeant major out to replace him to maintain continuity. Indeed, the British specially assign senior-level mentors for each of the operational squadrons.

Such an approach may fill a critical gap seen across a number of units. In the particular case of commandos, an ODA captain is typically assigned the responsibility of mentoring a battalion commander. Interviews at CJSOTF-A suggest there are concerns that the O-3–O-5 rank gap is too great, given cultural concerns of Afghans. Indeed, it was offered that there might be a need to increase the rank of battalion mentors by assigning an O-4 major to each ODA to provide additional seniority and experience to the battalion mentor role. This is hindered, however, by a shortage of AOBs to fulfill this role and the controversy

---

Box 7.6. Keep Your Promises

Keeping promises is as important in Afghanistan as it is in the United States, but it is made harder by short rotations and the lack of repeat rotations. Mentors had twice promised a bright Afghan Commando captain a nomination to Special Forces Q School, only to drop the ball and never follow through. Afghan command culture is very relationship-driven, and broken promises will diminish respect for a foreign military. In this case, the mentor was pushing paperwork to follow through on this promise, leaving a better relationship for the next rotation. If you cannot do it yourself, be careful not to promise it.

it may stir up because it is a nontraditional ODA employment scheme that has significant doctrinal implications.

We offer two possible approaches that might be used on a trial basis. First, a potential stopgap option would be to utilize chief warrant officers in this position. Their age, seniority, and status as officers may make them more suitable than team captains. Another advantage is that chief warrant officers can focus on the mentoring role without being encumbered by the need to plan and direct operations.

Second, and again as an experiment, an O-4 mentor could be assigned as the primary battalion commander/staff mentor for a SOK. This would free up the ODA captain (or captains) to focus on preparing his counterparts at the company level. This has significant doctrinal ramifications and therefore should be approached with caution. Nevertheless, we believe it merits exploration.

Continuity and Training

Maintain Effective Continuity of Operations

Continuity of operations is critical to success. Oftentimes, the risk is that new units conduct a RIP, forgo the practices of prior units, and instead forge ahead with new partnering practices and approaches identified during the PMT period. In the words of one senior officer at CJSOTF-A, new teams inevitably come in and "reinvent the wheel." Furthermore, absent a proper indoctrination on the status of their partner unit, the incoming unit is often predisposed to start training at baseline and so return to teaching basics already taught and learned. A recent RAND report on SOF continuity of operations addresses a number of key lessons learned derived from a case study on VSOs.[2] Many of the lessons identified during the course of the continuity study validate the observations of this analysis. That said, best practices from existing partnering operations suggest several critical courses of action.

---

[2] Todd Helmus and Austin Long, *Beyond the High Five: Managing Relief in Place at the Tactical and Operational Levels*, unpublished RAND Corporation research, 2013.

Return Units to Old Areas of Operations

First, it is critical that commands establish a rotation cycle that returns teams to their previously mentored units. The need for repeat tours was addressed previously as part of the discussion on partnership rapport. Beyond the rapport benefits, it appears from examples in Afghanistan, as well as the case study in Iraq, that rotations of new units to a partner force led mentors to unnecessarily retrain skills that had already been mastered. Of course it is important to note that there may be tension between this recommendation and the need for more-senior mentors for some units. For example, returning an ODA to the same SOK it partnered with previously would mean that the mentor for the SOK commander would still be a team captain. Yet careful and creative personnel assignments can manage these tensions. So, in this example, the senior mentor assigned could be a Special Forces major who, on a previous tour as an ODA team captain, had worked with the SOK commander.

Use Staggered Relief in Place

Second, staggered RIP seems to be important. Virtually all NMU mentor units employed a staggered RIP, with commanders arriving several weeks to a month before the main element of the unit. In this way, incoming commanders have an opportunity to witness the battle rhythm of the predecessor unit and carefully consider ways to integrate existing operational approaches into their future operational plans.

Ensure Proper Handoff of Information

Third, incoming teams must have a robust mechanism for procuring information on operations, the partner force, and partnership approaches from their predecessor units. Some standard practices, such as a PDSS, are critical in this regard, and are in fact followed across nearly all surveyed units. Prior to a unit's deployment, it should be in constant contact with the currently deployed unit through phone calls, emails, and routinely scheduled video teleconferences.

Follow a Multiyear Strategy

Fourth, it is critical that higher-echelon units provide proper oversight of unit continuity. Suggesting a best practice that can be applied across all SOF units, several coalition units employed multiyear written strategies that sought to promote partnership continuity. The Norwegians, for example, employed a milestone plan for evaluation. That document is modified, but maintained across rotations. It looks forward two to three years and is a tool for discussion between rotating units throughout the tour, as it is reevaluated every three months. The Lithuanians are also pursuing a multiyear strategy. This is especially critical for this contingent, as mentorship teams RIP in and out of Afghanistan every four months. They achieve continuity across these RIPs by following a long-term campaign plan so each rotation builds on its predecessors. The ISAF commander's intent provides the framework for the task force's goals. They also use the ISAF SOF commanders' conference and guidance from Joint Force Command Brunssum to help direct task force operations and influence lines of effort.

Ensure Proper Command Oversight on Continuity

Though not conveyed as a strategy per se, the British forces mentoring CF 333 and ATF 444 rely on their centralized headquarters in the United Kingdom. When units try something that works well, such as the creation of a new method for assessing CF 333 staff and squadron capabilities, the headquarters will tell the British mentorship to write it into policy. Guidance was reported as neither too detailed nor too vague. Though such efforts might seem to undercut operational freedom, it is actually welcomed by the British team mentoring CF 333. In this way, the British headquarters takes a direct role in helping to ensure continuity.

Properly Assess Partner Units

Finally, assessments play a critical role in continuity. As previously noted, the danger with RIPs is that new teams come in and feel they need to re-teach the basics. Part of this stems from ad hoc assessment approaches that are commonly employed. The most frequent assessment approach is to evaluate Afghan performance during individual operations and then re-focus training on areas deemed most immature. This approach may work during the course of a single deployment, but it does not allow assessment of improvements over time and across RIPs and does not allow comparative assessment of capabilities across multiple units. The former CJSOTF-A commander recognized this issue and noted that there needs to be a higher-level assessment that can carry over rotations and get passed during handover, so that the new unit can make progress rather covering the same ground.

We recommend a best practice observed at CF 333. When the new British partner unit deployed, it saw an opportunity to export an assessment method successfully used within the Royal Marines. These forces essentially rate each J-function on key performance tasks along an eight-point scale. The tasks and responsibilities for each section are broken down into key constituent parts. For example, the Afghan J-2 is assessed, in part, along the following lines:

> Integrates with Afghan J-2 structure and effectively obtains intelligence from them; . . . Identifies and articulates intelligence requirements, particularly for force protection purposes; Conducts information management; Analyses and assesses intelligence; Evidential exploitation; Processes detainees; etc.[3]

The assessment protocol also requires Afghans to provide self-assessments. This provides a feedback mechanism to help Afghans learn the critical staff process of unit capability assessment. It also gives the Afghans a broad-based understanding of performance areas in need of improvement. Of course, the Afghans may rate themselves too highly, but then the British use such inflated ratings as a means to further mentor the Afghans on the reality of their capability.

Pre-Mission Training

PMT that is focused on preparation for the partnering mission appears limited in scope. A number of units across the spectrum of the U.S. and ISAF special operations community appear to have a PMT curriculum that is primarily focused on conducting kinetic operations. In Iraq as well, training appeared to focus on direct action skills. While some Special Forces operators felt that this focus was sufficient because they are more oriented as a force to the FID mission, other Special

---

[3] Senior officer, mentor force, March 1, 2013.

Forces personnel, as well as SEALs, believed that a greater focus on training to train would have been beneficial.

In only a few cases did training appear to address the planned mentorship mission. In such cases, the primary approach was for SOF units to train conventional-force infantrymen as part of PMT. For example, some units preparing for partnered operations in Iraq used a mock partner force from the 101st Airborne Division. In Afghanistan, the Lithuanians conducted training exercises with members of their country's National Guard unit. Scenarios included the use of interpreters and simulated translations. They reported that this was excellent preparation for PRC operations. The ODA mentoring 1st SOK had a similar experience working with a conventional force reconnaissance squadron. The exercise capstone was a "combined" exercise that involved seizing an objective with an exfiltration akin to that frequently conducted in Afghanistan. Officers we spoke to were enthusiastic about the exercise, with one commenting that it was "some of the best training I ever had. They were doing the same thing we are doing now."

This recommendation echoes those presented in a 2012 report on lessons learned from the preceding decade, prepared by the Joint and Coalition Operational Analysis division of the Joint Staff J-7. One of the lessons highlighted in the report is the importance of host-nation partnering, and among the recommendations it provides to improve partnership is to renew focus on preparing units for partnership. It argues that the Defense Department should

> [r]e-establish a Military Assistance and Training Advisory . . . course to promote effective partnering and advising. This course should capitalize on recent lessons and Special Forces expertise with regard to FID and [security force assistance] operations.[4]

This Military Assistance and Training Advisory course (or courses) could provide exactly the sort of preparation for partnership that many SOF units would benefit from before deployment.

---

4   Joint and Coalition Operational Analysis, *Decade of War, Volume I: Enduring Lessons from the Past Decade of Operations*, Suffolk, Va.: Joint Staff J-7, June 15, 2012, p. 34. We thank David Maxwell for highlighting this report and recommendation.

CHAPTER EIGHT

Conclusion: SOF Partnership Beyond Afghanistan

While the focus of this report has been primarily on Afghanistan, many of the general challenges and best practices are likely to be constant across efforts to build SOF partner capacity. However, specific situations will vary greatly. Therefore, we conclude with four general observations based on the three cases reviewed here.

First, building partner capacity seems, inevitably, to take longer than anticipated.[1] This seems to be true whether the host nation is weak and international SOF are committed in large numbers (Iraq, Afghanistan) or the host nation is relatively strong and international SOF are committed in small numbers (Colombia). It seems unlikely at best that large numbers of international SOF would be committed to an already relatively strong host nation, as SOF are scarce and tend to be committed where the situation is most dire. Expectations should therefore be tempered for how quickly SOF partner units will develop.

Second, there is a tendency, perhaps related to the desire to produce quicker results, to build partner-force "tooth" (operational combat units) much faster than "tail" (combat support and enablers). U.S. assets are then used to provide those tail functions, with the idea that those capabilities will be built later. Yet given the first observation, these capabilities end up being anemic for a long time and perhaps never develop. It would therefore seem to be better to emphasize building these capabilities much more in the beginning, accepting that this will reduce the speed of tooth development.

---

[1] This is echoed in Paul et al., 2013.

Third, given the time necessary to build SOF partner capacity and the importance of rapport to such efforts, it may be worthwhile to explore nontraditional or atypical assignments for U.S. SOF personnel. Just as one example, the British Army has long seconded officers to certain Gulf States to help build capacity. These officers, typically senior field grades near the end of their careers, are seconded for long accompanied tours, typically four years.[2] While such an approach might not be suitable for host nations experiencing high levels of violence, it might be a much better use for many senior field grade SOF officers than a final tour as a Pentagon action officer.

Fourth, it is important to acknowledge that some international units are more readily able to effectively partner with host-nation SOF. This is due to organizational culture as well as differences in the nature of selection and training across SOF units. As noted in the Iraq case study, U.S. Special Forces often required less mental adjustment to become effective partners to host-nation SOF than U.S. SEALs. This is due to the greater emphasis of Special Forces on FID missions, while SEALs focus much more on direct action and special reconnaissance.

This divergence is not unique to U.S. SOF. There is variation both across and within many other international units in terms of the ease of adjustment to partnership. For example, there is some anecdotal evidence that there is a similar variation with Polish SOF, with some direct action–oriented units facing similar challenges in adjusting their mindset to partnership.[3] Planners and policymakers must acknowledge and remain cognizant of these differences as they align SOF units with missions.

---

[2]   Conversation with seconded British officer, April 2013.

[3]   Conversations with Polish SOF personnel, Afghanistan, July–August 2013.

Interview Protocol

Overview: The RAND Corporation is an independent and non-profit think tank based in Santa Monica, California. This study is sponsored by NATO Special Operations Component Command–Afghanistan (NSOCC-A)/SOJTF-A. The study seeks to capture the varying approaches NSOCC-A undertakes to build Afghan special operations capacity, identify lessons learned, and craft recommendations for improved Afghan partnership.

From February 24 to March 10, RAND researchers will conduct two BFCs [battlefield circulations] in Afghanistan (in both the east and south) that will enable brief embeds across ANA Special Forces, ANA Commandos, and General Directorate of Police Special Units (GDPSU), including Provincial Response Companies. RAND analysts will interview U.S. and coalition mentors and partnered units, observe unit training, and collect relevant lessons learned/after-action reports. RAND will further support this study through interviews with CONUS [continental United States]-based SOF units. RAND will also conduct case studies of SOF partnership from Operation Iraqi Freedom and U.S. assistance to Colombian Armed Forces.

Points of Contact: This partnership study is led by Dr. Austin Long. He can be reached at al2866@columbia.edu or Long@rand.org. The RAND lead for NSOCC-A Support, Dr. Todd Helmus, can be reached at helmus@rand.org and helmus@wdc.rand.pentagon.smil. mil.

Sample Interview Protocol: All interviews will be cited anonymously. Participation in this study is voluntary.

1. What were the strengths and weakness of your pre-mission training in preparing you for this partner mission? What would you improve?
2. How would you describe your unit's approach to SOF partnership?
3. What is the ultimate goal of your current partnership in terms of partner-force capability?
4. What is the greatest obstacle to your current partnership?
5. In what areas (if any) has your partner unit improved during your current rotation?
6. What are the strengths and weaknesses of your partner unit? In what areas are improvements most needed and how would you make these improvements if you had more time?
7. What techniques did you use to build rapport with your partner unit? How effective were they?
8. Did you or members of your unit have prior experience with your partner unit? If so, what effects (positive and/or negative) did that have?
9. How do teams best transition responsibility for partnership to their follow-on unit?

References

9010 Reports—*See* U.S. Department of Defense, "Report to Congress: Measuring Stability and Security in Iraq."

Arango, Tim, "Syrian War's Spillover Threatens a Fragile Iraq," *New York Times*, September 24, 2012, p. A1. As of August 9, 2013:
http://www.nytimes.com/2012/09/25/world/middleeast/iraq-faces-new-perils-from-syrias-civil-war.html?ref=world&_r=0&pagewanted=all

Bremer, L. Paul, "Coalition Provisional Authority Order Number 2," *IraqCoalition.org*, May 23, 2003. As of August 9, 2013:
http://www.iraqcoalition.org/regulations/20030823_CPAORD_2_Dissolution_of_Entities_with_Annex_A.pdf

Brennan, Richard, Jr., Charles P. Ries, Larry Hanauer, Ben Connable, Terrence K. Kelly, Michael J. McNerney, Stephanie Young, Jason Campbell, and K. Scott McMahon, *Ending the U.S. War in Iraq: The Final Transition, Operational Maneuver, and Disestablishment of United States Forces–Iraq*, Santa Monica Calif.: RAND Corporation, RR-232-USFI, 2013. As of August 14, 2014:
http://www.rand.org/pubs/research_reports/RR232.html

Butler, Dave, "Lights Out: ARSOF Reflect on Eight Years in Iraq," *Special Warfare*, January–March 2012.

Center for Civil Military Relations, "Responses to Maritime Security" workshop, Monterey, Calif., Naval Postgraduate School, September 6–10, 2010.

Chappell, Bill, "Iraq Battles Militants for Key Oil Refinery in Beiji," *NPR*, June 19, 2014. As of August 1, 2014:
http://www.npr.org/blogs/thetwo-way/2014/06/19/323524324/iraq-battles-militants-for-key-oil-refinery-in-baiji

"Colombia Trains Mexican Pilots," *Diáglo*, January 1, 2013. As of April 20, 2013:
http://www.dialogo-americas.com/en_GB/articles/rmisa/features/knowledge_is_power/2013/01/01/feature-pr-15

Entous, Adam, Julian Barnes, and Siobhan Gorman, "CIA Ramps Up Role in Iraq," *Wall Street Journal*, March 11, 2013.

Gordon, Michael, and Bernard Trainor, *The Endgame: The Inside Story of the Struggle for Iraq, from George W. Bush to Barack Obama*, New York: Random House, 2012.

Helmus, Todd, and Austin Long, *Beyond the High Five: Managing Relief in Place at the Tactical and Operational Levels*, unpublished RAND Corporation research, 2013.

Human Rights Watch, "Colombia," in *World Report 2013*, 2013, pp. 214–221.

International Crisis Group, "Loose Ends: Iraq's Security Forces Between U.S. Drawdown and Withdrawal," Middle East Report no. 99, October 26, 2010. As of August 9, 2013:
http://www.crisisgroup.org/~/media/Files/Middle%20East%20North%20Africa/Iraq%20Syria%20Lebanon/Iraq/99%20Loose%20Ends%20-%20Iraqs%20Security%20Forces%20between%20US%20Drawdown%20and%20Withdrawal.pdf

"Interview: General Martin Carreno," *Jane's Intelligence Review*, March 2004.

Isacson, Adam, *Consolidating "Consolidation": Colombia's "Security and Development" Zones Await a Civilian Handoff, While Washington Backs Away from the Concept*, Washington, D.C.: Washington Office on Latin America, December 2012.

Joint and Coalition Operational Analysis, *Decade of War, Volume I: Enduring Lessons from the Past Decade of Operations*, Suffolk, Va.: Joint Staff J-7, June 15, 2012.

Joint Publication 1-02, *Department of Defense Dictionary of Military and Associated Terms*, Washington, D.C.: U.S. Department of Defense, November 8, 2010 (as amended through July 16, 2014).

Joint Publication 3-22, *Foreign Internal Defense*, Washington, D.C.: U.S. Department of Defense, July 12, 2010.

Jones, James, *The Report of the Independent Commission on the Security Forces of Iraq*, Washington, D.C., September 6, 2007. As of August 9, 2013:
http://csis.org/files/media/csis/pubs/isf.pdf

Long, Austin, "Partners or Proxies? U.S. and Host Nation Cooperation in Counterterrorism Operations," *CTC Sentinel*, November 30, 2011. As of August 12, 2014:
https://www.ctc.usma.edu/posts/partners-or-proxies-u-s-and-host-nation-cooperation-in-counterterrorism-operations

"Los Militares Estan Perdiendo la Guerra," *El Timepo*, April 23, 1998.

Marcella, Gabriel, *The United States and Colombia: The Journey from Ambiguity to Strategic Clarity*, Carlisle, Pa.: U.S. Army War College Strategic Studies Institute, May 2003. As of August 11, 2014:
http://www.strategicstudiesinstitute.army.mil/pubs/display.cfm?pubID=10

Marks, Thomas A., *Sustainability of Colombian Military/Strategic Support for "Democratic Security,"* Carlisle, Pa.: U.S. Army War College Strategic Studies Institute, July 2005. As of August 11, 2014:
http://www.strategicstudiesinstitute.army.mil/pubs/display.cfm?pubID=610

————, "Colombian Crossroads," *Soldier of Fortune*, September 2001.

Marshall, Tyrone, "Building Allied Capability, Capacity Best Approach, McRaven Says," *American Forces Press Service*, April 9, 2013.

McDermott, Jeremy, "Green Berets Move into Colombia," *The Daily Telegraph* (UK), October 12, 1998.

————, "Colombia Imposes Democratic Authority," *Jane's Intelligence Review*, October 2002.

————, "USA Faces Colombian Dilemma," *Jane's Intelligence Review*, April 2003.

————, "Colombian Insurgency Escalates as Guerrillas Go Back on Offensive," *Jane's Intelligence Review*, July 2005.

————, "Destination Victory," *Jane's Intelligence Review*, July 2007.

Noggle, Michael R., "Senegalese and Malian Soldiers Train with U.S. Special Forces in Mali," Special Operations Task Force-103 Public Affairs press release, May 17, 2010.

Nossiter, Adam, Eric Schmitt, and Mark Mazetti, "French Strikes in Mali Supplant Caution of U.S.," *New York Times*, January 13, 2013.

O'Brien, Michael, "Foreign Internal Defense in Iraq: ASOF Core Tasks Enable Iraqi Combating-Terrorism Capability," *Special Warfare*, January–March 2012.

Office of the Special Inspector General for Iraq Reconstruction, *Iraqi Security Forces: Special Operations Program Is Achieving Goals, but Iraqi Support Remains Critical to Success*, Arlington, Va., SIGIR 11-004, October 25, 2010.

Paul, Christopher, Colin P. Clarke, Beth Grill, Stephanie Young, Jennifer D. P. Moroney, Joe Hogler, and Christine Leah, *What Works Best When Building Partner Capacity and Under What Circumstances?* Santa Monica, Calif.: RAND Corporation, MG-1253/1-OSD, 2013. As of August 11, 2014:
http://www.rand.org/pubs/monographs/MG1253z1.html

Plummer, Don, briefing to SOF Academic Week–OEF XXI, May 28–31, 2013.

Rabasa, Angel, and Peter Chalk, *Colombian Labyrinth: The Synergy of Drugs and Insurgency and Its Implications for Regional Stability*, Santa Monica, Calif.: RAND Corporation, MR-1339-AF, 2001. As of August 11, 2014:
http://www.rand.org/pubs/monograph_reports/MR1339.html

Rasheed, Ahmed, and Oliver Holmes, "Prisoner Deaths Indicate Mass Executions by Iraqi Police," *Reuters*, June 27, 2014.

Rathmell, Andrew, Olga Oliker, Terrence K. Kelly, David Brannan, and Keith Crane, *Developing Iraq's Security Sector: The Coalition Provisional Authority's Experience*, Santa Monica, Calif.: RAND Corporation, MG-365-OSD, 2005. As of August 11, 2014:
http://www.rand.org/pubs/monographs/MG365.html

Restrepo, German Giraldo, *Transforming the Colombian Army During the War on Terrorism* Carlisle, Pa.: U.S. Army War College, March 2006.

Salisbury, Steve, "Colombian Crack Troops," *Soldier of Fortune*, April 1999.

Shifter, Michael, "Colombia at War," *Current History*, Vol. 98, No. 626, 1999.

United States Institute of Peace, *Civil Society Under Siege in Colombia*, Washington, D.C., Special Report 114, February 2004.

U.S. Department of Defense, "Report to Congress: Measuring Stability and Security in Iraq," Washington, D.C., various dates.

———, *Progress Toward Security and Stability in Afghanistan*, Washington, D.C., April 2014. As of August 12, 2014:
http://www.defense.gov/pubs/April_1230_Report_Final.pdf

U.S. Department of State, "International Military Education and Training," Washington, D.C, undated. As of July 10, 2013:
http://www.state.gov/t/pm/65533.htm

U.S. Office of Management and Budget, "Overseas Contingency Operations," in *Fiscal Year 2013 Budget of the U.S. Government*, 2012, pp. 89–92. As of August 11, 2014:
http://www.whitehouse.gov/sites/default/files/omb/budget/fy2013/assets/budget.pdf

West, Bing, *The Strongest Tribe: War, Politics, and the Endgame in Iraq*, New York: Random House, 2008.

Zirnite, Peter, "The Militarization of the Drug War in Latin America," *Current History*, Vol. 97, No. 618, 1998.

Zucchino, David, "America's Go-to Man in Afghanistan's Oruzgan Province," *Los Angeles Times*, January 13, 2013.